Organic By Choice

A (Secret) Rebel's Guide To Backyard Gardening

Maat van Uitert | FrugalChicken

Copyright © 2017 Maat van Uitert

All rights reserved. No part of this publication may be reproduced, stored in a retrieval system, or transmitted, in any form or in any means – by electronic, mechanical, photocopying, recording or otherwise – without prior written permission.

ISBN-13: 978-1545528112
ISBN-10: 154552811X

Thanks for buying Organic By Choice:
The (Secret) Rebel's Guide To Backyard Gardening!

As a Special Thank You, you can download your FREE companion guide:

Tomato Fever: Common Tomato Diseases & Their Cures

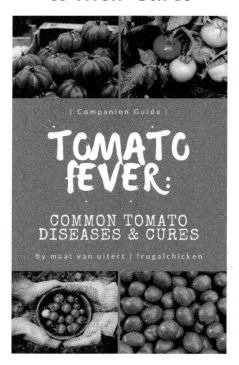

To get it, visit:
TheFrugalChicken.com/TomatoFever

Contents

Introduction: An Organic Rebel is Born 1

Part 1: Planning Your Organic Rebel Garden 5

Chapter 1: The Organic Rebel In Action (That's You!) 7

Chapter 2: Gardening Tools For The Organic Rebel 11

Chapter 3: The Organic Rebel's Garden Planning Guide 15

- Deciding on size 16
- Choosing a location 17
- Don't be shady: Give enough sun 17
- Sketching your garden plan 18
- Getting down & dirty with your soil 19
- Simple tests to determine your soil type 20
- Testing soil pH 21
- Improving clay or sandy soil for better harvests 22
- Sun worshippers versus shadier types 24
- Going over to the dark(er) side: Growing plants in shade 24
- Shedding light on light: 25
- Sample Gardening Plans 26

Chapter 4: It's Ok To Be Square
(Foot Gardening, That Is) 29

- Planning Your Square Foot Garden 30
- Raised Beds 34

Chapter 5: The Organic Rebel's Companion Planting Guide 39

v

Part 2: The Organic Rebel's Seed Starting Strategy Plan 49

  Chapter 6: Direct Sowing Seeds 51

    How to direct sow seeds 52

    Early Harvests & Succession Planting Choices 52

  Chapter 7: Starting Seeds Indoors 53

    What you need to start seeds indoors 53

    Homemade Organic Potting Soil Recipe 54

    When to start seeds 54

    How to start your own seeds 55

    Hardening off 57

  Chapter 8: What To Plant & Harvest By Month & Zone 59

**Part 3: The Organic Rebel's Plant Encyclopedia
& Growing Guide 85**

  Chapter 9: Veg Head: Vegetables & Legumes 87

    Vegetables 87

  Chapter 10: Fruits of Your Labor 113

  Chapter 11: Herb Delight 123

Part 4: Nurturing Your Garden Organic Rebel Style 141

  Chapter 12: Composting Guerillas 143

    Cold composting 143

    Hot composting 144

    Building a compost bin 145

    Creating compost in your kitchen with red wrigglers 146

    How to build a worm composting bin 146

  Chapter 13: Water, Water Everywhere 149

    The 6 commandments of watering 150

    Additional strategies to retain moisture 151

Watering schedule based on vegetable type: 152

Chapter 14: Homegrown Organic Fertilizers Rebel-Style 153
Understanding how fertilizers work 153
Using Banana Peels 154
Chicken manure tea 156
Rabbit manure 157
Seed meal fertilizer 157
Seaweed fertilizer 158
Homemade Fish Emulsion Fertilizer 158

Chapter 15: Bee Cool: Attracting Pollinators 159
Bees 160
Butterflies 162

Chapter 16: Self-Sufficient Water With Rain Barrels 169
What to look for in a rain barrel 170
Installing Your Rain Barrel 171

Chapter 17: Something Different: Using Essential Oils
for Companion Planting 173
Mixing oils to use in your garden 174
Guide to Vegetable & Essential Oil Companions 175

Chapter 18: Easier Gardening with Hay Bales 177
What is hale bale gardening? 177
How to prepare your hay bale garden 178
Planting your hay bale garden 179

Chapter 19: Weed Control, Organic Rebel-Style 181
Options for organic weed control 181
Organic weed control spray 184

Chapter 20: Organic Pest Control 185

Options for Organic Pest Control 185

Beneficial Organisms 188

Guide to Preventing Pests Based on Species 189

All-Natural Bug Spray 193

Garlic Pest Control Spray 193

Essential oils to repel garden pests 194

Protecting yourself with Gardener's Delight
Organic Fly Repellent 197

Part 5: Gardening in the 4th Season 199

Chapter 21: Extending Your Growing Season 201

Cold Frames 201

Hot Beds 206

Chapter 22: Gardening Over Winter 207

Garden clean up 207

Cover crops 208

Chapter 23: Growing Indoors 211

Herbs 211

Sprouts 212

Microgreens 213

Organic Seed Sources 215

References 217

Introduction: An Organic Rebel is Born

If thy heart fails thee, climb not at all.

~ Queen Elizabeth I

I'm sitting in my office in Silver Spring, Maryland where I've worked for the U.S. Government for the past 6 years. I'm in a meeting with my supervisor, a man who wanted to be liked—and liked to play games—and wanted nothing more than to end the conversation. For the third year in a row, he gives me a passive-aggressive excuse why I won't be considered for a promotion. Oh, and why he can't increase my bare-bones workload. In fact, the reason I can't be considered for a promotion is because they hadn't given me enough work in the past year to even judge my performance. This aggravating conversation went on for 2 more years, as I tried in vain to grow sweet potatoes and a single ripe tomato on my 2 foot by 5 foot porch—a hilariously hopeful experience I'll never forget.

About 30 minutes away, on the Fort Meyer, Virginia Army base, my husband had also been passed over for a promotion. He'd been told he could try to be promoted to Sergeant; the first time he'd tried, he had been given almost no time to prepare for the oral exam he'd have to undergo. A year later, when he met me, he had been promised for the fourth time he would be able to try for the promotion again—except shock of shocks, they weren't opening up the opportunity. In fact, they were happy with him, right in the position he already had.

At first opportunity, after our son was born, and we realized we were keeping the house to keep the jobs, and keeping the jobs to keep the house, we left our six-figure jobs and headed for our homestead, bent on living a healthy, organic life. As we looked back at the Beltway growing ever smaller in the distance, there was something taking it's place. A rebel was born.

As you read this story, I'm guessing you can relate. The organic life calls to some—and it's a call that's difficult to ignore. To be an organic gardener, however, I think you have to be a bit of a rebel. Even though the strategies in this book are as old as agriculture itself, there's nothing easy about sprouting seeds, trying to get rid of pests without modern chemicals, and sucking it up and trying, yet again, when vine borers have killed our squash harvest for 3 years straight. The grit to pursue this lifestyle is the stuff of Titans.

This book is a manual so you can start your organic life—beginning with the heart of this lifestyle, the garden. It's a wholesome, rewarding lifestyle—and definitely not for those whose hearts fail them easily. It's not a straight path to success,

Introduction: An Organic Rebel is Born

it's fraught with many turns and twists, so the road looks more like a child's scribble than a road to a full harvest. But it's the path that defines us—and makes us better gardeners!

I hope you enjoy this book, and it helps you yield a full table, a cabinet stuffed full of mason jars, and memories you'll giggle at and knowledge you can pass down to your grandkids.

Warmly,

Maat

Part 1: Planning Your Organic Rebel Garden

Chapter 1:
The Organic Rebel
In Action (That's You!)

Organic gardening has been around since humans put the first seeds into the ground and discovered agriculture. However, since World War II, when farming began to become industrialized, it's become a radical concept, shoved to the outskirts of the mainstream. Until now.

Organic gardening as a concept is really simple. You just grow your garden using all-natural solutions, making sure to keep chemicals far away. Before modern agricultural practices, people grew food without the use of chemicals. The early settlers of our country certainly didn't have Round-up! It only makes sense that we should be able to apply the same traditional techniques our ancestors used to produce the same results.

But the interest in organic gardening goes beyond just the benefits for us and our families. There has been a rise in the interest of ecology and concern about the environment that has given new life to this form of gardening. By using natural materials, by taking advantage of natural organisms, and by recycling garden waste, the home gardener can grow a wholesome, organic garden quite successfully.

Organic = Healthy Lifestyle

There are many, many advantages to gardening organically. Probably first and foremost is that food produced using organic agriculture is more nourishing and healthier. In early August, 2001, a British organization, *The Soil Association*, (https://www.soilassociation.org) reported that there's significant differences between organically and non-organically grown food. These differences relate to food safety, primary nutrients, secondary nutrients, and the health outcomes of the people who eat organically.

Vitamin C and dry matter contents are higher, on average, in organically grown crops than they are in non-organic crops, as well as mineral contents[7]. Food grown organically contains "substantially higher concentrations of antioxidants and other health promoting compounds than crops produced with pesticides." Plus, organically grown foods just taste better! If you've never tasted a fresh, organic tomato, you'll understand when you bite into one!

Overall, though, most people who enjoy organic gardening report that the enjoyment they derive is paramount to their decision to forget chemicals in favor of the organic route. Many people like to watch the tender new greens come to full maturity and, as a bonus, you get to eat it!

Part 1: Planning Your Organic Rebel Garden

For any gardener who still hasn't been convinced about the need to garden organically, here are some scary statistics that may change your mind:

In 2015, the World Health Organization said that herbicide glyphosate (commonly sold as Round-up) is "probably carcinogenic."[1] Herbicide glyphosate also has been said to be linked to Non-Hodgkins Lymphoma[8].

With the EPA's decision to phase out out of common pesticides such as Dursban and Diazinon[2], we are now realizing that many of the chemicals that we thought were "safe" were never actually tested to see what their effect on humans could be. In fact, many of these weed-killers are anything but safe. The time has come to reassess our dependence on pesticides.

Chapter 2: Gardening Tools For The Organic Rebel

The right tools for gardening will make your experience more enjoyable. Here's a list of tools to consider:

Spade

A sturdy spade, a short-handled shovel with a flat, squared-off blade, is essential. It's ideal for working soil amendments into the garden.

Fork

A garden fork loosens soil, let's you dig around plants, and moves mulch.

Gloves

Gloves will keep your hands cleaner and will help avoid blisters. Select garden gloves that have reinforced knuckles.

Hoe

A hoe is perfect for moving soil, creating planting furrows, breaking up clumps, and removing weeds.

Trowel

Trowels are perfect for planting herbs, transplants, and other small plants. Consider a trowel with a rubber handle, which will make it easier to hold for long periods.

Watering Hose

It's important to choose the right hose as it's one of the most critical gardening tools. It can quickly become a pain to maneuver, so make sure you buy a hose long enough to reach around your entire garden. Rubber hoses have the longest life and are least likely to kink, even if they're more expensive.

Drip system

A drip irrigation system allows you to water your plants more frequently by dripping or spraying. With it, you're able to keep roots moist more consistently, which is especially important during the hottest days of summer. You can find how to build a drip irrigation system at my friend Rick Stone's website, Our Stoney Acres http://ourstoneyacres.com/pvc-drip-irrigation-system-garden.

Rain barrels

Rain barrels aren't strictly necessary but they can make watering easier and cut down on your bills. We cover how to choose and install rain barrels in Chapter 16: Self-Sufficient Water With Rain Barrels.

Chapter 3: The Organic Rebel's Garden Planning Guide

Organic gardens perform much better when you make a strategic plan of where you'll plant your crops. Plants have natural defenses, and with companion planting and a little foresight, you can strategically make sure your vegetables grow in as healthy of an environment as possible.

Your first task when it comes to planning your garden is to figure out what USDA Zone you live in. This information will influence a lot of your decisions, including (but not limited to!):

- ❏ What crops you'll grow (it will be hard growing oranges in Minnesota!)
- ❏ When you will start your seedlings
- ❏ Your first & last frost date (influences when you transplant seedlings)

If you don't know your planting zone, you can find out on the USDA website at http://planthardiness.ars.usda.gov/. Once you know which zone you reside in, your next step is choosing where you'll plant your garden.

Deciding on Size

The next step to plan out your garden is to decide on a size. Of course, this will likely be determined by how large your property is. Whatever you decide, it's most important to not grow a garden that's too big for you to easily tend; many gardeners make the mistake of biting off more than they can chew. You don't want your garden to overwhelm you, because then you will give up as weeds and sweat get the better of you.

As a rule of thumb, if you have enough space, a good-size beginner vegetable garden is 14 feet by 10 feet. With a plot this size, you will have room for a variety of garden staples, and with luck, you'll have enough food to feed your family fresh vegetables for a few months.

For example, you will have enough room for:

- ❑ 6 tomato or 5 squash plants
- ❑ 5 pepper plants
- ❑ Peas and beans

You can grow potatoes and herbs in containers. Don't forget that you will also likely be growing different vegetables in the early spring, such as radishes, spinach, and lettuce, and tomatoes, squash, and pepper in the summer. During fall, you can try kale, parsnips, and other cool-weather-loving vegetables. Once you get the hang of growing produce, you can add more plants so you have leftovers to can and preserve.

Part 1: Planning Your Organic Rebel Garden

CHOOSING A LOCATION

When choosing a location for your garden, there's factors you need to consider, including the amount of sun the site receives, what your soil type is, which vegetables you want to grow, and the amount of light those vegetables need. In this chapter, there's a table that lists the amount of light each vegetable and herb type requires to grow.

For most vegetables, the site needs to get at least 6 hours of direct sunlight daily. The soil should be fertile, loamy, and should drain well, with no standing puddles. The area should receive adequate air circulation, yet be protected from strong winds. Your house, a tall fence, or a group of trees can act as a shield from the wind.

DON'T BE SHADY: GIVE ENOUGH SUN

When planning your garden, it's important to make note of sunny and shady areas. Some plants, no matter how hard you try, will not grow in shade simply because they aren't getting enough sun to thrive. It's critical to know not just whether a particular area of your garden is sunny or shady; it's also important to take note of how MUCH sun a particular plant needs to survive. So how do we define a sunny spot versus a partially sunny spot versus a partially shady spot?

Sunny: Areas that get more than 6 hours of sun per day. Even if the area is shady during part of the day, if it gets at least 8 hours of sun, it's still considered "full sun."

Part sun: A spot that gets 4 to 6 hours of sun per day.

Shady: A spot that gets less than 3 hours of sun a day.

Fully shaded: A spot that receives no direct sun. Not advised for growing vegetables.

SKETCHING YOUR GARDEN PLAN

Once you've chosen your site, draw out a garden plan; this plan will ensure maximum productivity by giving each plant room to grow. To draw out a plan:

1. Measure the dimensions of the plot you have in mind.

2. Draw in any existing permanent features, such as fencing.

3. Make a note of sunny spots in your garden and shady spots; check several times throughout the day. Remember that a sunny spot in April may turn into a shady spot in August; as you get to know your garden, you will understand how the season effects the available light.

4. List out the vegetables you plan to grow.

5. Consult the companion planting guide (Chapter 5, The Organic Rebel's Companion Planting Guide) to make sure you don't accidentally put the wrong plants next to each other.

6. Draw a scale model on graph paper, using, for example, a 1-inch square to represent 1 foot of garden space.

As you draw your plan, keep in mind each plant's space requirements at maturity. The little tomato plants you put out in the spring will take up much more space by the end of summer. Something to consider is Square Foot Gardening (see Chapter 4: It's Ok To Be Square (Foot Gardening, That Is). Because you don't have to allow as much space for paths, this will enable you to plant more.

The layout of your garden partially depends on what vegetables or fruit you want to plant. Some crops, such as lettuce, radishes, and spinach mature quickly and will be short-term residents, unless you plant and harvest them several times during the summer. Other plants, such as tomatoes, eggplant, and peppers, will grow over the course of the entire season. Perennial herbs and flowers will remain in the same spot year after year, requiring an increasing amount of space each passing season.

Another key to growing a healthy garden is to choose plants suited to the site. Plants adapted to your climate and conditions are better able to grow without a lot of attention or input; on the other hand, when you try to grow a plant that is not right for your site, you will probably have to boost its natural defenses to keep it healthy and productive.

Once you plan out your garden for this year, consider making a plan for next year as well, since it's best to rotate crops every year. Because crop rotation is so important to keep soil healthy and reduce potential diseases, as long as you're making a plan for the current year, draw up plans for the following year as well.

Getting down & dirty with your soil

As you plan out your garden, it's important to know what kind of soil you have. There's three types of soil: Clay, sandy, and loamy. This information will tell you whether you need to amend your soil, and increase your chances of a successful harvest. You also will have a better idea which plants will grow well in your garden.

Clay soil

Clay soil is comprised of small particles and tends to be heavy, packed tightly, and difficult for gardening. It drains slowly, holds little water and little air. You will need to amend clay soil, or consider raised beds.

Sandy soil

Sandy soil is comprised of particles that are loose and large. Unlike clay soil, it drains well, but loses moisture and nutrients quickly. You will have to fertilize frequently because your plants will not get much nourishment from the soil. In warm climates, it can also radiate heat, making it difficult to grow cold-loving crops.

Loamy soil

Loamy soil is ideal since it's a well-balanced mixture of clay, silt, and sand. It retains both moisture and nutrients to feed your plants well. If your garden has clay or sandy soil, you want to amend it so it will be as close to loamy as possible.

Simple tests to determine your soil type

Squeeze test

To easily figure out what soil you have, there's a simple test you can perform at home. Completely wet your garden site, then let it dry for a day. The following morning, pick up a handful of soil and squeeze it firmly. If the soil in your hand remains in a tight ball and is slippery, then it's clay soil. If the soil is gritty and doesn't hold its shape when squeezed or crumbles, it's sandy soil. If the soil stays in a loose ball when squeezed, your soil is loamy.

Jar test

If you want to try a different test, you can try the jar test. Take soil samples from several areas of your garden and mix them together. Take about 1 cup of this soil mixture and allow it to dry overnight. When it's crumbly, crush it completely so it resembles a powder, and pour 1 to 2 inches into a mason jar. Add enough water to fill the mason jar ¾ of the way to the top.

Allow the soil to settle completely in the jar; this might take a few days, so don't get discouraged. Eventually, the soil will settle into layers. You will see a difference in the size of particles—sand has large particles, loam has smaller, and clay is even finer. Once settled, look at the different layers of soil. Which layer is largest? The size of each layer determines whether you have mostly sand, loam, or clay soil. If your dirt is mostly loam - congratulations! If it's sand or clay, however, you will have to amend it.

Testing soil pH

Before amending your soil, you first need to know the pH. If your soil is too acidic or too alkaline, your plants won't be able to utilize the nutrients available. For most vegetable plants, a pH of 6.3 to 7 is ideal (in Chapter 9: Veg Head: Vegetables & Legumes, we get more specific by vegetable type). To determine the pH of your soil, it's best to send a sample to a soil testing lab. (You can use a home kit (http://thefrugal-chicken.com/soiltest), but they can be misleading, especially if the test is old.) A soil testing lab will also provide up-to-date recommendations for adjusting the pH of your soil. Be sure to remind them to only suggest organic methods. You can use those recommendations, as well as the recommendations in this book, to amend your soil.

Improving clay or sandy soil for better harvests

If you have clay or sandy soil, you will have to amend it. While clay soils are usually richer in nutrients than sandy soils are, it still can be difficult to grow vegetables in both soil types. Here's how to improve each, but remember, if you really run into trouble or aren't interested in taking the time to amend your soil, you always have the option to build raised beds.

Clay soil

To amend clay soil, you can add 2 to 3 inches of compost, worked into the soil to break it up, increase aeration, and improve water retention. In addition, you can mulch with organic materials like grass clippings or shredded leaves, which will then decompose, adding nutrients to the soil by default. A third option is to use a cover crop, such as winter wheat, red clover, or oats. Sow after your garden has been harvested for the year. When you're ready to plant the following year, just cultivate your cover crop into the soil to add more organic matter to your garden. Over time, your clay soil will turn to healthy, loamy soil. See Chapter 22: Gardening Over Winter for a detailed discussion of cover crop choices and planting options.

Sandy soil

Sandy soil does not hold nutrients or water well. An easy way to amend this type of soil is with 4 inches of compost. Till into the soil 6 inches deep before planting. Once you have planted your vegetables, keep them well-mulched with additional organic matter such as composted leaves or dry grass to conserve water. As the mulch breaks down, it will continue to add organic matter to the soil.

If your soil is sandy and you don't get much rain, be careful to choose plants that are drought-tolerant for the first couple years to improve your chances of a harvest. Examples include eggplant and many types of herbs. Once the soil is less sandy, you can try growing plants that are more sensitive to drought such as tomatoes.

Another option to improve sandy soil is to use charcoal (not grilling charcoal, but charcoal from agricultural byproducts such as corn stalks, straw, manure, animal bones, or wood). In studies, charcoal was shown to improve nutrient retention in sandy soil, create an environment that fosters beneficial microbes, and increase water retention.[6]

To add charcoal to your sandy soil, mix charcoal or coal dust with composted livestock or chicken (not cat, dog, or human) manure at a ratio of 1:3. Add 2 inches of the charcoal/manure mixture to your soil and till to a depth of 4 inches.

Sun worshippers versus shadier types

Sun plant: Needs more than 6 hours of sun each day.

Partial sun plant: Needs 4 to 6 hours of sun per day, but will tolerate more shade than a plant that needs full sun.

Partial shade plant: Will tolerate 4 hours of sun, but does well with shade during the hottest parts of the day.

Shade: Should not receive more than 3 hours of sun per day.

Going over to the dark(er) side: Growing plants in shade

- ❏ If possible, plant in containers that allow you to move the plants so they get more daily exposure to sun.

- ❏ Most herbs will tolerate partial shade. If possible, use them in shady areas so your vegetables get the necessary amount of light.

- ❏ Choose vegetables or herbs that will grow in shade; don't try to grow crops that require full sun if your yard is partly shady.

Part 1: Planning Your Organic Rebel Garden

SHEDDING LIGHT ON LIGHT:

Plant	Will tolerate:
Arugula, chard, kale, lettuce, mustard, spinach, bok choy, scallions	Partial sun
Beets, radishes, turnips	Partial sun
Broccoli, cauliflower, Brussels sprouts	Partial shade
Cabbage, kohlrabi	Partial shade
Carrots, parsnips	Partial shade
Celery	Partial shade
Garlic	Partial shade
Leeks	Partial shade
Peas	Partial shade
Potatoes	Partial shade
Tomatoes	Full sun
Cucumbers	Full sun
Melons	Full sun
Peppers	Full sun
Corn	Full sun
Beans	Full or partial sun
Squash	Full sun
Eggplant	Full sun
Basil, chervil, chives, lemon balm, mint, parsley, rosemary	Partial shade
Onions	Partial sun

Sample Gardening Plans

By now, you might be a bit overwhelmed, so in this section, we're going to look at different gardening plans. These are real-world gardens you can copy and recreate at home. In these plans, each vegetable or herb type has it's own "section," represented by a block in the table. If you don't like a particular vegetable, feel free to swap it for one you love—just be sure you consult the Companion Planting Guide in this book so you choose a vegetable that agrees with its neighbors.

Simple Garden Plan:

Beans	Spinach*	Spinach*	Peppers	Peppers	Tomatoes
Parsley	Chard	Broccoli*	Kale*	Broccoli*	Basil
Tomatoes	Chard	Beets*	Lettuce*	Beets*	Tomatoes

*Swap with warm weather crops in May, when it's too warm for cool-weather crops.

Cool Weather Garden:

Cabbage	Chard	Lettuce	Spinach	Kale	Broccoli
Cabbage	Chard	Lettuce	Spinach	Broccoli	Kale
Cabbage	Beets	Radishes	Radishes	Beets	Beets

*Alternatives: Peas, Bok Choy, Tatsoi, Kohlrabi

Summer Kitchen Garden:

Tomatoes	Tomatoes	Tomatoes	Beans	Eggplant	Squash
Basil	Rosemary	Thyme	Beans	Eggplant	Cucumbers
Squash	Squash	Squash	Peppers	Peppers	Cucumbers

Part 1: Planning Your Organic Rebel Garden

ABUNDANT HERB GARDEN:

Lemon Verbena	Rosemary	Basil	Basil
Sage	Cilantro	Thyme	Lavender
Bee Balm	Oregano	Oregano	Marjoram

*Be sure to leave your mint potted, otherwise it will take over the garden!

SALSA GARDEN:

Onions	Cilantro	Peppers	Tomatoes
Onions	Cilantro	Peppers	Tomatoes
Onions	Scallions	Jalapeno	Tomatoes

KID'S FUN GARDEN:

Tomatoes	Cucumbers	Melon	Corn
Tomatoes	Cucumbers	Melon	Corn
Eggplant	Tiny Pumpkins	Squash	Beans
Peas	Tiny Pumpkins	Squash	Beans

Chapter 4:
It's Ok To Be Square
(Foot Gardening, That Is)

You've probably heard of square foot gardening. In this chapter, you'll learn how to use it advantageously to grow organic vegetables right in your own backyard, with less space, cost, and effort. Square foot gardening is a type of intensive gardening in which you divide your garden into 12-inch by 12-inch squares; in each square you grow a different vegetable variety. You can grow more than one plant in each square, and the amount of plants in a square is dependent on the plant's size. You can grow a square foot garden in either the ground or raised beds.

Square foot gardening works well for a backyard organic rebel because it's more efficient, more cost-effective, and reduces weeds. It also can reduce diseases and pests. It's also space-saving; while a more traditional garden might take up your entire backyard, a square foot garden might only take up a quarter of the same space.

PLANNING YOUR SQUARE FOOT GARDEN

Similar to creating a traditional garden, you will also need to plan out your square foot garden. Ask yourself: How big will your garden be? Will you grow in the ground or on a raised bed? What vegetables or fruits do you want to grow?

When does each variety need to be planted? For example, you don't want to plant tomatoes in February when you can plant kale. Write down when each vegetable or fruit needs to be planted in your garden, as well as the length of time each needs to grow to harvest size.

DECIDING WHAT TO PLANT IN EACH SQUARE

When it comes to square foot gardening, you can't think about your vegetables as you would if you planted them in rows. Square foot gardening is intensive gardening, so you will plant vegetables closer together than you would in a traditional garden. Don't look at your seed packet for spacing directions; they're not relevant for square foot gardens.

Think of your vegetables in sizes; small, medium, large, and extra large. Small vegetables need to be 3 inches apart in your square foot garden, such as radishes, carrots, and beets. Plant up to 16 of these vegetables per square foot. Medium-sized vegetables need to be 4 inches apart, such as onions and garlic, and you can plant up to 9 of them per square foot. Plant 4 large vegetables, such as leaf lettuces and tomatoes, 6 inches apart in each square. Finally, extra large vegetables such as broccoli, need to be 12 inches apart, and you should plan on just 1 of them per square.

Also consider the size of each plant. You will want to take into consideration the amount of sun each plant needs to grow and whether they require support from a trellis (such as cucumbers or peas). Typically, in the United States, you will want to plant your taller plants, such as corn, to the North so they do not shade the shorter plants, such as lettuce. Additionally, plants that need the support of a trellis should be grown in a portion of your garden where the trellis will not interrupt the sunlight of shorter plants.

Finally, look at each vegetable type you will grow, and make sure it can be planted next to it's neighbor. Companion planting (Chapter 5: The Organic Rebel's Companion Planting Guide) is at the heart of square foot gardening, so consult a guide before finalizing your plans. You also want to make sure your vegetables won't be competing for space. For example, you don't want to plant sweet potatoes, with their sprawling vines, next to onions or melons! On the other hand, you can plant a heavy nitrogen feeder next to a more self-sufficient plant, and both have the opportunity to grow well. Consider placing plants side by side that help each other grow. For example, you can grow a vegetable that's susceptible to aphids next to a plant that repels the tiny pests. Your entire garden will benefit.

Example square foot garden plan:

Squash	Eggplant	Eggplant	Basil	Tomato	Tomato	Tomato	Squash
Thyme	Peppers	Collard	Collard	Lettuce	Lettuce	Peppers	Cukes
Parsley	Garlic	Garlic	Beets	Beets	Beans	Beans	Cukes
Thyme	Rosemary	Basil	Radishes	Radishes	Carrots	Carrots	Dill

PLANTING OPTIONS FOR SQUARE FOOT GARDENS

Plant	Number per Square Foot
Basil	4
Beans	8
Beets	9
Broccoli	1
Carrots	16
Celery	1
Chives	9
Cilantro	9
Collards	1
Corn	2
Cucumbers	2
Dill	1
Eggplant	1
Garlic	4
Kale	2
Leeks	4
Lettuce	4
Okra	1
Onions	4
Oregano	2

Part 1: Planning Your Organic Rebel Garden

PLANTING OPTIONS FOR SQUARE FOOT GARDENS CONTINUED

Plant	Number per Square Foot
Parsley	2
Parsnips	9
Peas	8
Peppers	2
Potatoes	1
Radishes	16
Rosemary	1
Spinach	9
Squash	2
Sweet Potatoes	1
Swiss Chard	4
Tomatoes	4
Turnips	9
Zucchini	4

Raised Beds

Raised beds versus traditional gardening

While both traditional gardening and raised beds have their pitfalls, there are some distinct advantages that raised beds have over traditional gardening, namely:

- ❑ More food in less space
- ❑ More successful harvests, because soil is more fertile
- ❑ Less competition from weeds
- ❑ Fewer pests

With raised beds, you can focus on growing vegetables in a small area, and you can work, water, weed, and fertilize more economically than you can with rows. It's also easier to use season-extending options, such as cold frames, cloches, and row covers.

Raised beds can be any height you desire, but they're most successful when they're 8 to 24 inches deep. The deeper the soil that's available to growing plants, the more room their roots have to grow, and the more nutrients they will have. Deep, fertile soil also holds moisture better.

You can establish your raised beds anywhere, as long as the site is permanent. Each year, you want to improve the soil, grow nitrogen fixers, and keep the soil healthy with cover crops during winter. If you constantly move your beds, you will always be working hard to establish good soil, instead of improving on it. You can construct beds on poor or compacted soil, sand, or even on concrete—one farm we lived on before our homestead constructed raised beds out of cinder blocks,

How many raised beds are enough?

It's easy to go overboard and build a garden too big for you to maintain; it's also easy to underestimate how much space you need. So, how many raised beds should you construct?

First start with your goals. What do you want to grow? How much of it? Do you want enough to feed your family for the entire year? And do you have the space for that? What about the time? Even if you don't want to grow very much now, what about in a year? 5 years?

Look at your growing area. How many square feet is it? How large will your raised beds be? If your time and space is limited, or if you're brand new to gardening, it's best to start with just one or two raised beds.

Another consideration is cost. To construct your raised beds, you will need to either source free timber, or purchase materials to build them. You will also need to purchase or otherwise source organic soil and compost, or make and transport your own. Price your materials, and from there, determine how many beds you can afford to create.

Location, location, location

Next, look at your garden location. For the best results, most of your plants will need at least 8 hours of full sun daily. Your raised beds will bed to be in an area with constant access to sun. You'll want to have easy access to a hose, since most plants in your garden will need an inch of water each week.

Soil for your raised beds

Next to sun, good soil is the most important ingredient for a healthy, growing garden. After you construct your raised beds, you will need to fill it with soil that's loose, fertile, and rich with nutrients and organic matter. You can use purchased soil, or a mix of soil on your property plus a healthy dose of compost mixed in.

You will want to test the pH of your garden at your county agricultural extension. You CAN use an at-home soil testing kit, but they can yield incorrect results. The tests performed by your local agricultural extension will be accurate. Before constructing your raised beds, remove any grass or weeds from the area. Loosen the soil on the build site to a depth of 6 inches to improve drainage and moisture retention.

Wood considerations

Raised beds are easy to make, can be made quickly, and can last season after season. If your raised beds will be a permanent feature in your yard, you will want to use materials that can withstand the elements. Most people use wood to make their raised beds, and you can either buy brand new wood or source heat-treated pallets (look for the HT stamped on the pallet to ensure it's heat-treated and safe to use in a garden). When it comes to pressure-treated wood, some gardeners are concerned about safety. In the United States, chromated copper arsenate (CCA) pressure-treated wood has been banned since 2002[9], so any pressure-treated wood you buy at a local store will not contain arsenic.

If you do not want to use pressure treated wood at all, you do have options. Cedar, with natural oils to withstand wind, rain, and mold, is one option, especially since many common garden pests shy away from it. If you use wood for your raised beds, use 2-inch thick boards to ensure an even longer life. A second option is to use concrete to build your raised beds. Concrete can increase the pH of your soil, so be sure to test your soil each year. Bricks or naturally-found rocks are a third and fourth option.

Plans you can follow

Our raised beds are 5 feet wide and 10 feet long. The advantage to these dimensions is you can purchase wood inexpensively in 10-foot lengths, simply cutting one piece in half for the shorter sides. You can also make your beds 4 feet wide by 8 feet long, or any other dimension that fits your yard. Just make sure you can access your plants without stepping into the bed.

While the depth of raised beds can vary, 6 inches is a minimum, and 12 to 24 inches is ideal. It's deep enough without being so deep that it's labor-intensive and expensive to purchase organic soil and compost to initially fill it up. Most plants need at least 6 to 24 inches for roots.

While not strictly necessary, if you have stubbornly healthy grass or weeds, consider lining the bottom of your bed with fabric or digging down several inches into the soil to ensure no weeds can creep into your carefully-tended raised bed.

Supplies for a 12-inch deep raised bed:

- ☐ (6) 2x6 cedar or pressure-treated pine boards in 10-foot lengths, 2 boards cut into 5-foot lengths
- ☐ (1) 5 pound box of 4-inch wood screws
- ☐ (1) 2x4, 8 feet long, cut into 12-inch lengths

Directions for Constructing a Raised Bed:

Construct your raised bed in its permanent location. Using the 12-inch sections of the 2x4 as vertical braces in each corner, construct your raised bed. Screw the 10-foot sections to the braces, and then screw the 5-foot long end pieces to the 12-inch braces, forming the raised bed.

Chapter 5: The Organic Rebel's Companion Planting Guide

Before drawing your garden, consult this guide to companion planting. It will guide you so you don't make a critical error that might ruin your harvest!

Basil

Plant near: Any other crops

- ❏ Improves the flavor and growth of garden crops, especially tomatoes and lettuce. Repels mosquitoes.

Bush Beans

Plant near: Beets, cabbage, carrots, catnip, cauliflower, corn, cucumbers, potatoes, savory, strawberries

Don't plant near: Fennel, garlic, leeks, onions, shallots

Pole Beans

Plant near: Corn, radishes, marigold, potatoes

Don't plant near: Beets, garlic, kohlrabi, leeks, onions, shallots

Beets

Plant near: Broccoli, brussels sprouts, bush beans, cabbage, cauliflower, chard, kohlrabi, onions

Don't plant near: Mustard, pole beans

Borage

Plant near: Squash, strawberries, tomatoes

Borage repels tomato worms. Improves flavor and growth of companions.

Broccoli

Plant near: Beets, dill, calendula, carrots, chamomile, mint, onions, rosemary, sage, thyme

Don't plant near: Strawberries

Brussels Sprouts

Plant near: Beets, calendula, carrots, chamomile, dill, hyssop, marigolds, mints, onions, rosemary, sage, thyme

Don't plant near: Strawberries

- ❏ Marigolds repel cabbage moths.

Cabbage

Plant near: Broccoli, brussels sprouts, celery, chard, spinach, tomatoes

Don't plant near: Strawberries

- ❏ Tomatoes and celery repel cabbage worms.

Cauliflower

Plant near: Broccoli, brussels sprouts, celery, chard, spinach, tomatoes

Don't plant near: Strawberries

Carrots

Plant near: Cabbage, chives, early potatoes, leeks, lettuce, onions, peas, radishes, rosemary, sage.

- ❏ Onions & leeks repel carrot flies

Chives

Plant near: Berries, carrots, grapes, peas, tomatoes

- ❏ Chives improve flavor and growth of companion plants, deters aphids and Japanese beetles

Corn

Plant near: Beans, cucumbers, potatoes, melons, peas, pumpkins, squash

Cucumbers

Plant near: Beans, cabbage, corn, early potatoes, radishes, sunflowers

Don't plant near: Potatoes

- ❏ Radishes deter cucumber beetles. Cucumbers encourage blight in potatoes.

Dill

Plant near: Broccoli, brussels sprouts, cabbage, cauliflower, cucumber, lettuce, onions

Don't plant near: Carrots

- ❏ Dill improves flavor and growth of cabbage, cauliflower, lettuce.

Eggplant

Plant near: Pole beans, peppers, potatoes, tomatoes

Green beans deter potato beetles.

Garlic

Plant near: Cabbage, cane fruits, fruit trees, roses, tomatoes

Don't plant near: Peas, beans

- ❏ Garlic deters Japanese beetles and aphids. Garlic tea might repel potato blight.

Kale

Plant near: Herbs, cabbages

Don't plant near: Strawberries, beans

Lettuce

Plant near: Beets, carrots, parsnips, radishes, strawberries

Don't plant near: Cabbages, cauliflower

- ❑ Lettuce can make radishes more tender.

Marigold

Plant near: All garden crops

- ❑ Marigold stimulates vegetable growth and deters bean beetles, aphids, potato bugs, squash bugs, and maggots.

Marjoram

Plant near: All garden crops

- ❑ Marjoram helps vegetables grow better, keeps away pests.

Mustard

Plant near: Fruit trees, grapes, legumes

- ❑ Mustard stimulates growth of companion plants.

Nasturtiums

Plant near: Beans, cabbages, potatoes, pumpkins, radishes, squash

- ❏ Nasturtiums repel aphids, potato bugs, squash bugs, whiteflies.

Onions

Plant near: Beets, lettuce, carrots, cabbages, chamomile, parsnips

Don't plant near: Beans, peas

- ❏ Onions deter most pests.

Oregano

Plant near: All garden crops

- ❏ Oregano deters pests and enhances flavor of companion plants.

Parsley

Plant near: Corn, tomatoes

Helps improve flavor of companion plants.

Parsnips

Plant near: Onions, radishes

- ❏ Onions keep root maggots from destroying parsnips.

Peas

Plant near: Beans, carrots, corn, cucumbers, potatoes, radishes, turnips

Don't plant near: Leeks, onions, shallots

Peppers

Plant near: Basil, carrots, eggplant, onions, parsley, tomatoes.

Don't plant near: Fennel

Potatoes

Plant near: Basil, beans, cabbages, corn, eggplant, peas, squash

Don't plant near: Apples, birch, cherries, cucumbers, pumpkins, raspberries, tomatoes, walnuts

- ❑ Basil deters potato beetles. Marigolds deter nematodes.

Radishes

Plant near: Chervil, cucumbers, lettuce, melons, peas

- ❑ Radishes deter cucumber beetles. Chervil makes radishes hot. Lettuce helps make radishes tender.

Rosemary

Plant near: Beans, cabbage, carrots

- ❑ Rosemary repels bean beetles, cabbage moths, and carrot flies.

Sage

Plant near: Cabbages, carrots, tomatoes

Don't plant near: Cucumbers

Sage deters cabbage moths and carrot flies, and stimulates growth in tomato plants.

Spinach

Plant near: Celery, cauliflower, eggplant, strawberries

Strawberries

Plant near: Beans, lettuce, borage, spinach

Don't plant near: Cabbages

Squash

Plant near: Corn, peas, melons, beans, marigold, nasturtium

Tarragon

Plant near: All garden crops

- ❑ Tarragon can improve vegetable flavor and growth.

Thyme

Plant near: All garden crops

- ❑ Thyme deters cabbage moths.

Tomatoes

Plant near: Asparagus, basil, cabbages, carrots, mustard, parsley, onions, rosemary, sage

Don't plant near: Fennel, kohlrabi, potatoes, walnuts

Part 2: The Organic Rebel's Seed Starting Strategy Plan

Chapter 6: Direct Sowing Seeds

Some plants don't transplant well, and so you will want to direct sow them into the ground. Examples include radishes, most leafy green veggies, and carrots. When you direct sow seeds, however, remember they will take a little more time to grow to harvest size than transplanted starts. So direct sowing seeds that take 120 days or more to reach maturity, such as tomato, squash, and eggplant, means that you either need a long growing season or to use season extending covers.

Seeds have within them everything they need to grow, except moisture and warmth. When direct sowing, however, it's important to be careful you don't over or underwhelm your sprouting seeds. They should get enough light and be planted in the soil deep enough to provide warmth to urge the seeds to sprout, but not so deep they won't have a chance to grow.

How to Direct Sow Seeds

The rule of thumb is to plant your seeds to a depth of no more than 2 times their width; any more and you will likely not have any seedlings. Deep soil is heavy and cool (dig your finger 4 inches down in soil to see what I mean), and often damp enough to rot off the emerging leaf bud before it can break the surface.

Very fine seeds, such as turnip or lettuce seeds, only need a very light dusting of soil. One option is to broadcast these smaller seeds and scratch them into the soil (just remember you will likely have to thin later if you broadcast). Once they're in the ground, mark what you have planted where. We use a popsicle stick with the plant name written on the front and stick it in the ground at the beginning of the row. Mist well, but don't use direct pressure or you will displace your seeds. You'll soon begin to notice small plants popping through the soil and reaching for the sun. Before long, with proper cultivation, you'll have beautiful plants!

Early Harvests & Succession Planting Choices

If you want to plant vegetables for an earlier harvest, consider radishes, kale, and lettuce. They tend to come up quickly, and can be harvested before any of your other plants have even begun to set flowers. With these types of vegetables, plant a small bed and keep replanting every 2 or 3 weeks in small amounts. You'll take up the same amount of space, save harvest time, and have a continuous crop throughout the growing season.

Chapter 7: Starting Seeds Indoors

Most gardeners start their vegetables indoors and under lights so they can get a jump start on the growing season. You can use a spare room, your garage, or a greenhouse, anywhere that you can fit equipment, including a grow light. Starting your seeds indoors will decrease the amount of time you have to wait to see results in your garden. Just remember that when your seedlings are ready to be transplanted outside, you will have to harden them off.

What you need to start seeds indoors

In order to start your seeds indoors, you will need some supplies! Here's what you should have on hand:

- ❏ Potting Mix (commercial or homemade)
- ❏ Seed starting tray or peat pots (http://thefrugalchicken.com/tray)

- ❑ Plastic to cover the starting tray (http://thefrugalchicken.com/cover)
- ❑ Seeds
- ❑ Heat mat (http://thefrugalchicken.com/heatmat)
- ❑ Grow lights (http://thefrugalchicken.com/growlights)

Homemade Organic Potting Soil Recipe

You can buy organic potting soil, but if you're growing a lot of seedlings, the expense can be overwhelming. Plus, there's really no guarantee your soil will actually be organic unless you make it yourself. Here's a simple recipe to follow that you can create at home.

- ❑ 4 parts compost
- ❑ 1 part perlite (http://thefrugalchicken.com/perlite)
- ❑ 1 part vermiculite (http://thefrugalchicken.com/vermiculite)
- ❑ 2 parts coconut coir (http://thefrugalchicken.com/coir)

Lightly moisten each ingredient before mixing them, but don't soak them, since too much moisture can lead to damping off. (Damping off is a fungal disease that causes seedlings to die.) Add enough of the potting soil to peat pots so there's enough for your seedlings.

When to start seeds

The perfect time to start seeds will depend on a lot of factors, such as your last frost date for your area and the length of time it takes for a particular plant to grow to maturity. Most vegetables can be started 6 to 8 weeks before your area's last spring frost date. You can find a vegetable growing guide in Chapter 9: Veg Head: Vegetables & Legumes.

How to start your own seeds

Germinating seeds

Fill clean containers with a commercial or homemade seedling mix Chapter 7: Getting Ahead: Starting Seeds Indoors. Pour your seedling mix into a large bucket and moisten with warm water. Aim for just enough moisture so the mix retains its shape when squeezed in your hand. Plant your seeds according to the planting guide in in Chapter 9: Veg Head: Vegetables & Legumes. Most seeds can simply be gently pressed into the mixture; you can use a chopstick to push in seeds.

Almost any container with drainage holes in the bottom will work for planting. Peat pots are most popular. If you use seed trays or individual peat pots, place 2 or 3 seeds in each pot. Do not cover too deeply, as this may reduce or prevent seed germination. Cover containers with plastic or use a plastic top. This will retain moisture so your seedling mix doesn't dry out. Water your seedlings carefully, since too much water can cause damping off, displace the soil, or drown your seedlings. A mist sprayer is best.

Seeds sprout best at temperatures of 65 to 75 degrees F, depending on the variety. You can use a commercial heat mat or alternatively, find a place in your home where there are natural low levels of heat for the bottom of your seed tray.

Nurturing seedlings

When seedlings appear, remove the plastic and move containers under a grow light. Don't skip this step and try to use a sunny window, because there won't be enough light to grow strong seedlings. Your grow light can be a standard shop light outfitted with a fluorescent or daylight-simulating bulb. It's important to make sure you use a grow light to start seeds; without it, you run the risk of producing seedlings that are "leggy," meaning they're tall, weak, and unable to support themselves. If your plants get to this stage, you will likely have to start over because they will be too weak to grow to maturity and bear fruit.

Position the grow light about 1 inch above the tops of your seedlings. When the seedlings have developed the first true leaves (the leaves above the cotyledons or "seed leaves"), thin to one plant per container if using partitioned trays or peat pots. Use tweezers or scissors to pinch off unwanted seedlings rather than pulling them, to avoid disturbing the remaining seedling.

When the seedlings get their second pair of leaves, prepare individual pots. Move the seedlings carefully to the new pots with potting soil and compost, and water well. When transplanting, try to retain as much of the old soil as possible around the roots to reduce transplant shock. Keep pots out of direct sun for a few days to reduce shock.

Hardening off

About one week prior to transplanting your seedlings outside, gradually expose seedlings to longer periods outdoors. Start with 1 hour and work up from there. Do not start hardening of if temperatures are below 50 degrees. At the same time, reduce watering to a minimum as long as plants do not wilt to help the plants adjust without experiencing shock when you transplant them.

When it comes time for planting in the ground, it's best to start on a cloudy day, or in the evening to reduce shock. Carefully remove the plant from its container, making sure to keep the root ball intact. Bring the plant's original soil with it. Dig a hole in your garden slightly larger than the root ball, and fill the bottom with compost for continual feeding. Place the plant into the hole, and cover up the roots completely nearly to the bottom leaves. Mist gently to water, but water deeply.

Chapter 8: What To Plant & Harvest By Month & Zone

To make it easy, I've listed out what vegetables you can plant each month based on zone. Just remember that each zone isn't always ideal for planting all the time! If a zone is missing, it's because it's better to plan your garden than to plant that month.

January

Zone 6

Start onions, leeks, broccoli, cabbage, and cauliflower indoors under lights.

Zone 7

Indoors, start cabbage, lettuce, and broccoli, onion, and cabbage.

Zone 8

- ❑ Plant asparagus crowns, strawberry plants, and fruit trees.
- ❑ Transplant onions, cabbage, broccoli, and chard, covering with a row cover if cold weather threatens.
- ❑ Direct sow beets, carrots, radishes, bok choy, and peas
- ❑ Direct sow herbs.

Zone 9

- ❑ Sow peppers, tomatoes, and eggplant in pots filled with a homemade organic seed starting mixture.
- ❑ Direct sow carrots, broccoli, lettuce, spinach, cilantro, parsley, tatsoi, and bok choi.

Zone 10

- ❑ Sow pumpkins and winter squash directly in the garden
- ❑ Start cucumbers and watermelons
- ❑ Sow quick-maturing varieties of carrots, broccoli, cabbage, coriander, parsley, and dill.
- ❑ Plant heat-tolerant chicory, lettuce, and Swiss chard varieties, making sure they're shaded they stay cool when the weather warms and don't bolt.

February

Zone 4

Start onions, leeks, lettuce, and celery under lights.

Zone 5

- ☐ Start lettuce, celery, onions, leeks, and early tomatoes indoors under lights.
- ☐ Direct sow spinach and radishes outdoors under a row cover.

Zone 6

- ☐ Under lights, start onions, leeks, broccoli, cabbage, cauliflower, and Brussels sprouts.
- ☐ Start seeds of early ripening tomatoes under lights now.

Zone 7

- ☐ Set out transplants of lettuce, cabbages, and onions and be sure to cover them on cold nights.
- ☐ Direct sow radishes, lettuces, spinach, turnips, and peas.
- ☐ Start herbs indoors under lights.

Zone 8

- ☐ Plant potatoes 4 inches deep in warm soil.
- ☐ Direct sow leaf lettuces, collards, and other greens outdoors

Part 2: The Organic Rebel's Seed Starting Strategy Plan

Zone 9

- ❑ Start tomatoes, peppers, and eggplants indoors under lights.
- ❑ Direct sow radishes, spinach, carrots, peas, onions, and cabbages.

Zone 10

- ❑ Direct sow corn, cucumbers, beets, carrots, and radishes
- ❑ Set out transplants of hot peppers
- ❑ Start okra, purple hull peas, and sweet potatoes.

March

Zone 3

Start onion, tomato, cauliflower, cabbage, brussels sprout seeds under lights.

Zone 4

Start all of the veggies listed above PLUS pepper, and eggplant seeds indoors under lights.

Zone 5

- ☐ Start tomato, pepper, and eggplant seeds indoors under lights.
- ☐ Direct sow peas, lettuce, radishes, potatoes, and carrots outside

Zone 6

- ☐ Start tomato, pepper, and eggplant seeds indoors under lights.
- ☐ Broccoli, cabbage, and cauliflower starts can be moved outdoors under a cold frame.
- ☐ Plant your potatoes as soon as the soil is workable.

Part 2: The Organic Rebel's Seed Starting Strategy Plan

Zone 7

- ❏ Direct sow or transplant Swiss chard, carrots, beets, kohlrabi, radishes, leaf lettuces, onions, shallots, broccoli, cabbage, cauliflower, collards, white potatoes, asparagus crowns, and turnips.
- ❏ Place potted herbs outside, such as rosemary, chives, and thyme.

Zone 8

- ❏ Direct sow fast-maturing spinach, turnips, mustard, beets, carrots, and broccoli.
- ❏ Direct sow corn, tomatoes, squash, peppers, and cucumbers.

Zone 9

- ❏ Direct sow cabbage, broccoli, spinach, radishes, tatsoi, bok choy, lettuce, and parsley.
- ❏ Transplant tomatoes, peppers, and eggplants outside

Zone 10

Start okra, sweet potatoes, mustard, collards, cucumbers, and melons.

April

Zone 3

- ❑ Direct sow onions, lettuce, spinach, peas, carrots, and parsnips.
- ❑ Indoors, start squash, melons, and corn.
- ❑ Sprout seed potatoes by bringing them into room temperature.

Zone 4

- ❑ Direct sow peas, spinach, lettuce, radishes, and onion outside.
- ❑ Plant raspberries bushes
- ❑ Under lights, start tomatoes and broccoli

Zone 5

- ❑ Transplant early tomatoes outdoors
- ❑ Direct sow a second crop of lettuce and spinach

Zone 6

Plant potatoes, peas, spinach, beets, turnips, and carrots.

Part 2: The Organic Rebel's Seed Starting Strategy Plan

Zone 7 & 8

- ❑ Direct sow purple hull, crowder, and black eye peas, okra, squash, melons, cucumbers, and corn
- ❑ Start peanuts, sweet potatoes
- ❑ Start warm-loving herbs such as basil, thyme, and oregano

Zone 9

- ❑ Direct sow pumpkins, summer squash, and melons, bush beans, and corn

May

Zone 3

- ❑ Direct sow Swiss chard, spinach, lettuces, radishes, kale, and cabbages.
- ❑ If warm enough, start, beans tomatoes, summer squash
- ❑ Plant potatoes.

Zone 4

- ❑ Start melon, cucumber, and squash seeds indoors or in a coldframe.
- ❑ Direct sow tomatoes, beans, and summer squash

Zone 5

- ❑ Transplant peppers, melons, tomatoes, eggplants, cukes, and sweet potatoes.

Zone 6

- ❑ Plant peppers, tomatoes, and eggplants
- ❑ Direct sow squash, beans, corn, and okra.
- ❑ Sow sunflowers

Zone 7

Direct sow or transplant okra, tomatoes, eggplant, peppers, sweet potatoes, purple hull peas, and other heat-loving vegetables.

Zone 8

- ❑ Continue to plant heat-tolerant tomatoes.
- ❑ Transplant eggplant, peppers, cucumbers, squash, okra, beans, melons, peas, and sweet potatoes this month.

Zone 9

Start melons, squash, beans, okra, and purple hull peas.

Zone 10

- ❑ Plant heat-loving veggies, such as sweet potatoes, okra, and purple hull peas.

June

Zone 3

- ☐ Harden off, and set out transplants of melons, tomatoes, squash, peppers, cucumbers, and eggplant.
- ☐ Direct sow lettuce, radishes, and spinach every 2 weeks for a continuous harvest.

Zone 4

- ☐ Direct sow melons and squash.
- ☐ Direct sow more lettuce so you can keep harvesting.
- ☐ Direct sow or transplant cilantro, basil, thyme, and other herbs.
- ☐ Plant heat-loving tomatoes

Zone 5

- ☐ For an autumn harvest, plant bush beans, Brussels sprouts, and cabbage.
- ☐ Plant heat loving tomatoes and eggplants

Zone 6

- ☐ Transplant okra or a late crop of summer squash.
- ☐ Plant corn, beans, cucumbers, and sweet potatoes.

Zone 7

- ☐ Plant pole, lima, and bush beans; corn, black eyed peas, winter squash, and gourds.
- ☐ Start seeds in a greenhouse for fall harvests of eggplants, peppers, and tomatoes.

Zone 8

- ☐ Plant mustard to harvest tender baby leaves in 30 to 45 days.
- ☐ Plant fall crops of peppers and eggplant.
- ☐ Direct sow cantaloupes, corn, cucumbers, okra, peanuts, peas, summer squash, sweet potatoes, bush beans, and tomatoes for a fall harvest.

Zone 9

Plant sweet potato slips, peanuts, Swiss chard, and corn.

July

Zone 3

- ☐ Set out transplants of melons, tomatoes, squash, peppers, cucumbers, and eggplant.
- ☐ Direct sow lettuce, radishes, and spinach every 2 weeks for a continual harvest

Zone 4

- ☐ Direct sow heat-loving crops, such as tomatoes, melons, and squash.
- ☐ Direct sow lettuce, radishes, and spinach every 2 weeks for a continual harvest
- ☐ Direct sow carrots, broccoli, lettuce, tatsoi, spinach, cilantro, parsley, and bok choi.

Zone 5

For fall harvest, plant bush beans, Brussels sprouts, and cabbage.

Zone 6

- ☐ Direct sow okra, sweet potato slips, corn, beans, and cucumbers, or a late crop of summer squash.

Part 2: The Organic Rebel's Seed Starting Strategy Plan

Zone 7

- ❑ Plant pole beans, corn, lima beans, bush beans winter squash, and gourds.
- ❑ Start seeds in your greenhouse for fall harvests of eggplants, peppers, and tomatoes.

Zone 8

- ❑ Direct sow or transplant fall crops of peppers, cantaloupe, corn, cucumbers, okra, peanuts, southern peas, summer squash, sweet potatoes, eggplant, and bush beans.
- ❑ Direct sow tomatoes for fall harvest.

Zone 9

Plant sweet potato, corn, Swiss chard, and peanuts.

August

Zone 3

- ❏ Plant lettuce, turnips, parsnips.
- ❏ Save seeds from robust open-pollinated tomatoes and peppers.

Zone 4

- ❏ Plant lettuce and other fast-growing crops to replace those harvested.
- ❏ Save seeds from robust open-pollinated tomatoes and peppers.
- ❏ At month's end, direct sow spinach in a cold frame for a fall and spring harvest.
- ❏ Establish cover crops, such as clover, wheat, or barley.

Zone 5

- ❏ In your greenhouse, start lettuce and broccoli for a fall harvest.
- ❏ Transplant extra strawberry plants to a new bed.
- ❏ Direct sow carrots, beets, turnips, and radishes for a fall crop.

Zone 6

Direct sow lettuce, kale, spinach, and cabbage.

Part 2: The Organic Rebel's Seed Starting Strategy Plan

Zone 7

- ☐ Sow tatsoi, bok choy, radishes, beets, Swiss chard, and mustard.
- ☐ Set out fall transplants of broccoli, brussels sprouts, and cauliflower.

Zone 8

- ☐ Indoors, start broccoli, cabbage, and cauliflower.
- ☐ Transplant tomato and peppers.
- ☐ Direct sow corn, cucumbers, squash, and herbs such as basil

September

Zone 3

- ☐ Harvest corn, potatoes, apples, cucumbers, tomatoes, squash, and strawberries, and green tomatoes. Allow to ripen or make fried green tomatoes.
- ☐ After onion tops fall over, dig up, and let cure for 7 days before storing them.

Zone 4

- ☐ Plant spinach in a cold frame for overwintering.
- ☐ Protect plants from early frost with row covers.
- ☐ Look for dry pods on bean plants; save the seed for planting next season.

Zone 5

- ☐ Harvest green tomatoes
- ☐ Plant garlic for overwintering, making sure to put a heavy layer of straw over them when frost threatens.

Zone 6

- ☐ Get fall compost started with grass clippings, pulled plants, and leaves.
- ☐ Direct sow quick-growing cover crops such as winter rye or wheat.
- ☐ Direct sow spinach in cold frames for spring harvest.
- ☐ Plant garlic bulbs for harvest next summer.

Zone 7

- ❑ Direct sow lettuce, kale, turnips and other greens.
- ❑ Harvest herbs and dry or freeze them.
- ❑ Harvest peanuts as soon as shells become hard.

Zone 8

Direct sow or transplant broccoli, cauliflower, cabbage, spinach, lettuce, beets, carrots, parsley, turnips, kohlrabi, and kale. Be sure to cover dirt with mulch to cool the soil.

Zone 9

- ❑ Direct sow lettuce, peas, carrots, kale, bok choy, and tatsoi.
- ❑ Harvest winter squash and pumpkins before frost.

Zone 10

- ❑ Direct sow okra and herbs.
- ❑ Set out tomatoes, peppers, and onion transplants.

OCTOBER

Zone 3

- ☐ Harvest turnips, parsnips, and carrots if not overwintering.
- ☐ Harvest late apples.

Zone 4

- ☐ Harvest or heavily mulch carrots, beets, and other root crops.
- ☐ Plant garlic bulbs and shallots for a summer harvest.
- ☐ Sow a cover crop of winter rye or wheat to preserve soil.

Zone 5

- ☐ Compost asparagus beds.
- ☐ Direct sow spinach, kale, and cold-hardy lettuce.

Zone 6

- ☐ Direct sow spinach and other cold-friendly greens, under row covers or cold frames.
- ☐ Compost all spent plants, shredded leaves, and the last grass clippings.

Part 2: The Organic Rebel's Seed Starting Strategy Plan

Zone 7

- ☐ Thin radishes, carrots, and turnips sowed in September; then cover with an inch of very fine compost.
- ☐ Harvest sweet potatoes
- ☐ Plant garlic and direct sow spinach to overwinter

Zone 8

- ☐ Direct sow lettuce, bok choy, spinach, carrots, beets, peas, radishes, onions, turnips, garlic, and shallots.
- ☐ Sow a cover crop of winter rye, clover, or Austrian winter peas.

Zone 9

- ☐ Plant radishes, mustard, spinach, and turnips.
- ☐ Harvest sweet potatoes, winter squash, pumpkins, and peanuts.

Zone 10

- ☐ Plant tomatoes, peppers, and eggplants.
- ☐ Plant strawberries, broccoli, carrots, beans, parsnips, potatoes, sweet potatoes, lettuce, spinach, and other greens.

November

Zone 5

- ❏ Plant garlic and shallots 3 inches deep and 4-5 inches apart; mulch with 6 inches of straw.
- ❏ Harvest any remaining root crops.
- ❏ Dig the hole for planting live Christmas trees now, before the soil freezes.

Zone 6

- ❏ Thin lettuce and spinach, and mulch crops you want to overwinter with a thick layer of straw.
- ❏ Harvest Brussels sprouts, carrots, parsnips, cabbage, bok choy, tatsoi, and kale.

Zone 7

- ❏ Put lettuce, chard, spinach, chives, and parsley under cold frames before the first freeze.
- ❏ Plant new strawberries or move rooted runners.
- ❏ Feed leeks, then hill up soil around them to begin the blanching process.

Part 2: The Organic Rebel's Seed Starting Strategy Plan

Zone 8

- ❑ Plant fruit trees
- ❑ Harvest tomatoes, eggplant, and peppers
- ❑ Under cold frames, plant Brussels sprouts, cabbage, bok choy, tatsoi, broccoli, peas, carrots, kale, radishes, mustard, turnips, beets, and spinach.
- ❑ Plant cilantro, parsley, and fennel.
- ❑ Plant strawberries, mulch, and overwinter for spring/summer harvest

Zone 9

- ❑ Pick any remaining green tomatoes and allow to ripen indoors.
- ❑ Plant garlic, shallots, onion sets, and leeks.
- ❑ Harvest Brussels sprouts, broccoli, carrots, cabbage, turnips, and kale.
- ❑ Cover spinach and lettuce with row covers.

Zone 10

- ❑ Plant successive crops of cilantro, lettuce, radishes, and turnips.
- ❑ Harvest beans, peas, squashes, pumpkins carrots, cucumbers, early melons, and kale.
- ❑ Start tomatoes, peppers, and eggplant

December

Zone 5

Cover spinach, carrots, parsnips, and other overwintering crops with a cold frame.

Zone 6

Harvest leeks, kale, and any other cold weather crops.

Zone 7

- ❑ Add row covers to protect spinach, lettuce, and kale
- ❑ Plant bare root trees.

Zone 8

- ❑ Plant onions, chives, spinach, mustard, peas, beets, and radishes.
- ❑ Direct sow lettuce in a cold frame.
- ❑ Plant bare root trees and vines.

Zone 9

- ❑ Sow winter cover crops, including annual ryegrass, barley, wheat, or millet.
- ❑ Plant bare root trees and vines.

Zone 10

- ❏ Start cold-loving veggies, such as Brussels sprouts, kale, lettuce, radishes, and turnips.
- ❏ Harvest any citrus fruits, beans, beets, broccoli, carrots, greens, onions, potatoes, radishes, and melons.

Part 3:
The Organic Rebel's Plant Encyclopedia & Growing Guide

Chapter 9: Veg Head: Vegetables & Legumes

In this section, we'll cover best practices for growing common favorite vegetables, fruits, and herbs. To find out first and last frost dates for your area, visit http://www.almanac.com/gardening/frostdates/.

VEGETABLES

ASPARAGUS (ASPARAGUS OFFICINALIS)

Planting: Plant as soon as soil can be worked in spring. Pick a site in full sun with loamy, well-draining soil to prevent crown rot. Grows best in soil with a pH of 5.8 to 7. Start with 1 year old crowns for a faster harvest. Plant 18 inches apart in trenches 6 inches wide

and 6 inches deep. Cover crowns with 2 inches of soil. As plant grows, fill in trench slowly until only 4 inches of stem remain above soil. Mulch well after trench is filled.

Care: Hardy to Zone 4. Water regularly, but don't overwater. Side dress with compost each spring and fall. Susceptible to slugs, asparagus beetles, and cutworms.

Harvesting: Can take 3 years to produce a harvest. Don't harvest in plant's first year. Harvest lightly in the 2nd year, and only harvest spears thicker than ¼ inch. Cut at an angle. Produces over a 14 day period.

Beans (Phaseolus vulgaris)

Planting: Direct sow pole or bush varieties 1 inch deep and 2 inches apart after last frost date has passed and when soil is at least 50 degrees. Choose a well-draining site with loamy soil in full sun. Work a little compost into site, but don't over fertilize to avoid lush leaves with few beans. For pole beans, set up trellises before planting. Sow every 2 weeks for a continued harvest.

Care: Hardy to Zone 3. Requires full sun. Provide 1 inch of water weekly, making sure leaves remain dry to avoid mold. Mulch well to retain moisture. Side dress with compost when pods appear. Susceptible to aphids, Japanese beetles, Mosaic viruses, and white mold.

Harvesting: Harvest when pods are ripe. To harvest, snip off pods to avoid damaging plants.

Seed saving: Allow up to two pods per plant to mature for seed, if still harvesting fresh eating beans. If plant is for seed saving only, then all pods can be left to mature. Harvest seeds when pods have dried before rain; wetness can cause seeds to mold or sprout in their pods. Finish drying in indoors. Can keep for up to 4 years.

Beets (Beta vulgaris)

Planting: Direct sow in early spring or late summer in loose, well-draining soil, free of rocks. Ideal soil pH is 6 to 7. Broadcast, then cover with ½ inch of soil. Cover with a row cover to protect from frost. When seedlings emerge, thin to 3 inches apart.

Care: In early stages, side dress with bonemeal to improve roots. Needs full sun, but shade when hot to avoid bolting. Water consistently to avoid splitting. Mulch to retain moisture. Susceptible to leafminers, flea beetles, and leafhoppers.

Harvesting: For salad greens, harvest leaves 14 to 30 days after sprouting. Harvest roots before they reach 4 inches in size.

Seed saving: Beets flower and produce seeds in their second year. Overwinter 30 plants by mulching deeply with straw. Beets don't self-pollinate, and you need to have male and female plants. Can cross pollinate from up to 2 miles away; to ensure purity, bag plants in groups with wind-safe bags or plastic cages. After emerging the following spring, allow plants to flower and set seeds. To harvest, allow seeds to dry fully on the plants.

Bok Choy (Brassica rapa)

Planting: Direct sow 2 weeks before last spring frost date by broadcasting, then covering lightly with soil. Choose a site with loamy, well-draining soil, in partial shade to slow bolting.

Soil should be at least 50 degrees with a pH between 6 and 7.5. Thin to 6 inches apart.

Care: Keep cool, and mulch heavily to maintain moisture. Cover with plastic if frost threatens. Provide shade if temperatures rise.

Harvest: Harvest bok choy before temperatures rise, otherwise plant might bolt. Trim leaves as needed, leaving inner leaves alone for a continual harvest. When temps rise, harvest entire plant.

Seed Saving: Allow plants to bolt and flower. When the flowers form husks, wait until they turn brown and dry on the plant. Seeds are mature when the husk is dry and turns brown. Snip husk from plant and open to remove seeds.

BROCCOLI (BRASSICA OLERACEA)

Planting: Direct sow ½ inch deep or set out transplants 2 weeks before last frost date in spring or 100 days before first fall frost date. Soil temps must be at least 50 degrees. Choose a site in full sun, with loamy, well-draining soil. Space transplants or thin to 12 inches apart.

Care: Hardy to Zone 3. Needs full sun and cool temps. Side dress with compost 2 to 3 weeks after transplanting. Water well, avoiding heads. Mulch well to suffocate weeds and to keep soil cool. Susceptible to flea beetles, aphids, and downy mildew.

Harvesting: Harvest when the buds are closed and tight before flowers appear. Cut heads at a 45 degree angle.

Seed saving: Broccoli is not self-pollinating; you will need several plants to ensure pollination. To harvest seeds, allow heads to mature and turn yellow. Flowers will bloom, and create pods. Allow pods to dry on the plant. Do not allow pods to split open. When dry, pull plant and hang upside down to dry for 2 weeks. Open pods and remove seeds.

Brussels Sprouts (Brassica oleracea)

Planting: Start seeds indoors 8 weeks before last spring frost date or direct sow in full sun 4 weeks before last spring frost date. For fall harvest, direct sow 100 days before first fall frost. Direct sow ½ inch deep and space or thin to 12 inches apart. Before sowing or transplanting, amend soil with compost. Ideal soil pH is 7.

Care: Hardy to Zone 2. Needs full sun. Side dress with compost when plants are 5 inches tall. Mulch deeply to smother weeds, maintain moisture and cool soil in spring, or protect roots in fall. Pinch off top of plant as it matures to divert growth to sprouts. Susceptible to aphids, flea beetles, downy mildew, and white mold.

Harvesting: To harvest, trim 1-inch sprouts as they mature, checking plants every other day.

Seed saving: Requires pollination for fertile seeds, so plant several heads. If growing in fall, will need to over-winter, and flower the following spring. Allow plants to flower and produce seed pods. When pods are dry, remove from plant before they split.

Cabbage (Brassica oleracea)

Planting: Start seeds indoors 8 weeks before last spring frost date. Transplant 2 weeks before last spring frost date, spacing

24 inches apart. Choose a site with loamy, well draining soil in full sun. Avoid sites where cabbages were grown the previous year. Plant next to beans, dill, and cucumbers.

Care: Hardy to Zone 1. Needs full sun and cool temperatures. Side dress with compost 2 weeks after transplanting. Mulch well to keep soil moist, and water at least 1 inch per week. Susceptible to aphids, flea beetles, cabbage worms, cabbage root maggots, and cutworms.

Harvesting: Harvest by cutting heads at base with a knife when desired size. Remove entire plant at end of season to prevent soil-born diseases.

Seed saving: Requires pollination for fertile seeds, so plant several heads. If growing in fall, will need to overwinter, and flower the following spring. Allow plants to flower and produce seed pods. When pods are dry, remove from plant before they split.

Carrots (Daucus carota)

Planting: Direct sow 3 weeks before the last spring frost date. Plant by broadcasting seeds, then thinning to 4 inches apart. To thin, snip with scissors to avoid damaging remaining seedlings. Choose a site with full sun, loamy soil, free of rocks, and well-draining. Amend site with compost, but avoid manure because it can cause forked roots.

Care: Hardy to Zone 4. Requires full sun, water regularly but gently to avoid damaging tender seedlings. Mulch to retain moisture and suppress weeds. Side dress with compost 6 weeks after sowing.

Harvesting: Harvest when roots are ½ inch in diameter. If storing for winter, cover carrots with straw when a hard freeze threatens. Dig all winter as needed as long as ground isn't frozen.

Seed saving: Save seeds in the plant's second year. You will have to overwinter carrots under 6 inches of straw in Northern climates. When flowers emerge, allow to turn brown and dry. Seed heads should ripen and dry on the plant. When dry, snip from plant and place in a plastic bag to complete drying process.

CAULIFLOWER (BRASSICA OLERACEA)

Planting: Difficult to grow in gardens because cauliflower will not grow well if temperatures are not consistently in the 60s. To grow, start with transplants. Choose a site with 8 hours of sun, and a soil pH of 6.5 to 7. Amend soil with compost, transplant 2 weeks before the average last spring frost date, spaced 24 inches apart. For a fall harvest, plant 6 weeks in part shade before first frost date. Temperatures should be below 70 degrees consistently. If temperatures below 60 degrees threaten, cover plants with plastic.

Care: Requires full sun in spring, partial shade in warm fall weather. Mulch well, provide 1 inch of water per week. Side dress with compost when transplants are 3 weeks old. When heads are 3 inches wide, tie leaves together to cover the head to blanch. Susceptible to cabbage worms, aphids, and cabbage root maggots.

Harvesting: Harvest about 10 days after blanching by cutting heads off with a sharp knife. At end of season, pull entire plant out to avoid soil-borne diseases.

Seed saving: Requires pollination for fertile seeds, so plant several heads. If growing in fall, will need to over-winter, and flower the following spring. Allow plants to flower and produce seed pods. When pods are dry, remove from plant before they split.

Collards (Brassica oleracea,)

Planting: Plant seeds indoors 8 weeks before last spring frost date. Broadcast and thin to 18 inches apart when plants are 3 inches tall. Transplant outdoors 3 weeks before the last spring frost date. For fall harvests, direct sow 8 weeks before the first frost date. Choose a site with loamy, well-draining soil with a pH of 6.5 to 7, and in full sun. Will tolerate partial shade, especially during warmer weather.

Care: Hardy to Zone 6. Needs full sun in cool weather. Side dress with compost when plants are 4 inches tall. Provide 1 inch of water per week, mulch to keep soil cool and retain moisture.

Harvesting: Harvest collard leaves starting at the bottom and working up Best when leaves are young.

Seed saving: Will produce flowers in the plant's second year. Overwinter under 6 inches of straw. When plant flowers, allow seed pods to harden and dry on plant. Pull entire plant from garden, bag, and hang upside down to complete drying. Remove seeds by rubbing pods between your fingers.

Corn (Zea mays)

Planting: Extend harvest with early, midseason, and late varieties. Direct sow 2 weeks after last spring frost date in loamy, well-draining soil, when soil temperature is 70 degrees or higher. Ideal soil pH is 7. Plant 12 inches apart, in short but many rows to encourage cross pollination.

Care: Hardy to Zone 4. Needs full sun and warm temperatures. Corn is a heavy feeder, so side dress with compost. Provide 2 or more inches of water a week, especially during warm weather. Mulch to retain moisture. Susceptible to flea beetles and cutworms.

Harvesting: Harvest when white tassels turn brown and kernels swell. To harvest, twist ears off stalk.

Seed saving: Not self-pollinating, so plant in blocks to ensure pollination. Look for open-pollinated varieties for seed saving. To harvest seeds, allow ears to mature and dry on stalks. Harvest as soon as they are dry but before rain threatens. Allow kernels to continue to dry on husks indoors. When kernels are dry, rub of cobs with your fingers.

CUCUMBERS (CUCUMIS SATIVUS)

Planting: Start seeds indoors as early as 4 weeks before last spring date, using a heat pad to raise soil temp to 70 degrees. Transplant outside 3 weeks after last spring frost date. If direct sowing, choose a site in full sun with loamy, well-draining soil with a pH of 7. Direct sow seeds 1 inch deep and 12 inches apart at least 3 weeks after last spring frost date.

Care: Hardy to Zone 4. Not frost tolerant; don't sow if cold weather threatens. Requires full sun. Give 1 inch of water each week, especially during dry, hot spells. Mulch to retain moisture and keep cucumbers clean. Plant near flowers or a beehive to ensure pollination. Susceptible to mosaic virus, cucumber beetles, and whiteflies.

Harvesting: Harvest every other day to keep plant productive. Over ripe when fruit turns yellow. Slicing varieties should be 6 to 8 inches long, and pickling varieties 2 inches long. Look for firm, crisp cucumbers.

Seed saving: Leave cucumbers on vine until yellow or orange and no longer edible. Carefully cut and remove seeds. Place seeds in a bowl of room-temperature water. Allow to ferment for 3 days to remove outer coat and cucumber pulp. After 3 days, separate seeds from water. Toss seeds that float; they're not viable. Spread viable seeds on paper towels and dry thoroughly.

Eggplant (Solanum melongena)

Planting: Sow seeds indoors 8 weeks before transplant date. Seeds need soil temperatures above 75 degrees to germinate. When plants are 4 inches tall, harden off, bringing inside if temperatures drop below 60 degrees. Plant outdoors in full sun, 24 inches apart, when temperatures are consistently above 70 degrees, and water well. Soil pH should be between 6.5 and 7. Choose a location where eggplants, tomatoes, potatoes, or peppers were not grown for 2 or more years.

Care: Hardy to Zone 4. Needs full sun; cool temperatures can stunt fruit growth. Side dress with compost every 2 weeks. Keep watered, mulch to retain moisture. Susceptible to aphids, mites, tomato hornworms, powdery mildew.

Harvesting: Harvest late summer, when skins of fruit are shiny. To harvest, cut stems with a sharp knife.

Seed saving: Leave eggplants on plant (but off the ground) until brown or white and no longer edible. Carefully cut eggplant and scoop out seeds. In a fine mesh colander, separate seeds from pulp. Once separated, place seeds in water; remove seeds that float; they are not viable. Rinse and thoroughly dry viable seeds.

Jalapenos (Capsicum annuum)

Planting: Sow 8 to 12 weeks before the last spring frost date. Sow seeds in pots ½ inch deep. Cover lightly with soil. Use a heat mat so soil temperatures reach 80 degrees. Keep soil consistently moist, but don't overwater. As seedlings grow, keep temperatures at 80 degrees. Transplant outside in full sun, and in well-draining soil with a pH about 7, when temperatures are consistently above 75 degrees.

Care: Hardy to Zone 7. Needs full sun and conditions between 65 and 80 degrees. Water roots well, especially during dry spells. Don't water peppers to avoid mold. If temperatures dip, bring potted plants inside or cover with plastic.

Harvesting: Harvest when peppers are 4 to 6 inches long, firm, and a glossy green. To harvest, snip the stem.

Seed saving: Allow peppers to ripen and dry completely on plants. Harvest by snipping pepper from plant, and gently opening pod. Remove seeds and allow to dry for another 2 weeks indoors.

Kale (Brassica oleracea acephala)

Planting: Sow seeds outdoors as soon as soil can be worked by broadcasting, then thinning to 18 inches when plants are 4 inches tall. For a fall harvest, plant 60 days before the first fall frost date. Choose a site in full sun, with loamy, well-draining soil, pH 7 to 7.5.

Care: Hardy to Zone 3. Needs full sun, but will tolerate some shade. Give 1 inch of water each week, do not overwater. Mulch in spring to retain moisture and keep roots cool. Mulch in fall to protect roots and keep productive. Susceptible to cabbage worms, flea beetles, and aphids.

Harvesting: Harvest when leaves are 4 inches or more. Trim leaves from outside the plant, leaving new growth inside alone. Extend harvest by covering plants with row covers or a cold frame when temperatures reach below freezing. Kale will grow as long as temperatures don't dip below 20 degrees.

Seed saving: Allow plants to bolt and flower. For fall plantings, will have to overwinter under 6 inches of straw and allow to flower the following spring. Allow seed pods to mature and thoroughly dry on the plant. Harvest before pods drop seeds.

Leeks (Allium porrum)

Planting: For summer harvest, start from seed 8 weeks before the last spring frost date. For a fall/winter harvest, sow in April. Transplant 10 weeks after sowing. Choose a site in full sun, with loamy, well-draining soil, where onions or garlic have not grown for at least 2 years. Prepare site by tilling in 2 inches of compost, and plant 6 inches apart. Plant in a trench 6 inches deep, and mound soil up to the leaves.

Care: Hardy to Zone 7. Needs full sun, cold hardy down to 5 degrees F. Water consistently, and mulch well to retain soil moisture. Blanch leeks by continuing to mound soil around stem. Susceptible to slugs, leaf rot, and leek rust.

Harvesting: Harvest when stems are at least 1 inch in diameter. Harvest by pulling out of the ground; if leeks resist, loosen soil, and gently pull them out.

Seed saving: Allow leeks to flower and set seeds. When seeds are dark and flower turns brown, cut stalk. Place a paper bag over flower, securing with a clip or rubber band. Hang upside down indoors until seeds fall from plant.

LETTUCE (LACTUCA SATIVA)

Planting: Start seeds indoors 6 weeks before last spring frost date or direct sow seeds when temperatures outside are 45 to 70 degrees. Broadcast and cover lightly with dirt, or scratch seeds into soil and cover with plastic. Soil should be loamy, with a pH of 7, in full sun, and well-tilled. Transplant seedlings 2 weeks before last spring frost date. Sow every 2 weeks for a continued harvest. Space leaf lettuce 4 inches apart and firm-headed types 18 inches apart.

Care: Hardy to Zone 4. Water well, mulching to maintain moisture, suffocate weeds, and keep roots cool when temperatures rise. Side dress with compost 4 weeks after planting.

Provide shade and keep out of hot sun. Susceptible to aphids, cutworm, and white mold.

Harvesting: Harvest leaf types by trimming outer leaves when young, leaving inner leaves to mature. Overly mature leaves will be bitter, however. Harvest firm-headed types by cutting plants 1 inch above soil, leaving roots intact for a second harvest.

Seed saving: As plant flowers, allow seedheads to dry and harvest every other day. Plant will have flowers at various stages of maturity. Alternatively, wait until most of the flowers have seed heads, and remove entire plant. Place a paper bag over plant, securing with a rubber band or clip, and hang upside down until seeds fall.

Mustard (Brassica juncea)

Planting: Sow outdoors 3 weeks before your last spring frost date by broadcasting, then scratching into soil. Soil temperatures should be at least 55 degrees. Choose a site in full sun for chilly climates, in part sun with afternoon shade for warmer climates, with loamy, well-draining soil with a pH about 7. When seedlings appear, thin to 4 inches for greens, 6 inches for seeds. For fall/winter harvest, plant 8 weeks before first fall frost date.

Care: Hardy to Zone 4. Keep watered, but don't overwater. Mulch to retain moisture and keep roots cool in the heat, and protected in cold weather. Will bolt in the heat, so provide shade in warmer climates.

Harvesting: For greens, harvest by snipping leaves when 4 inches or longer. Younger leaves are most tender, will turn bitter if mustard bolts.

Seed saving: For seeds, harvest pods when they turn brown, after plant flowers. Remove seeds from the pods by placing flower heads in a bag. Pods will open in 7 to 10 days. Shake the bag to open pods.

OKRA (ABELMOSCHUS ESCULENTUS)

Planting: Best if direct sown, since roots are easily disturbed. Prior to planting, soak seeds in water for 12 hours to aid germination. Plant after last spring frost date, when soil is at least 65 degrees. Choose a site in full sun, with loamy, well-draining soil. Sow seeds 1 inch deep and 12 inches apart. Seedlings should appear in 14 days. Grows up to 6 feet, so can shade other plants.

Care: Hardy to Zone 7. Needs full sun, loves heat. Water regularly, especially when flowers appear and pods are developing. Mulch to retain moisture. Side dress with compost when flowers appear.

Harvesting: Harvest when pods are 3 to 4 inches long; any longer, and they will be tough. Can produce continuously for up to 12 weeks; check plants daily for pods, and pick regularly to keep plant producing.

Seed saving: Allow pods to dry on the plants until they crack. After pods are thoroughly dry, split them open and remove seeds. Spread seeds on paper towels, and allow to dry for an additional 2 weeks.

ONIONS (ALLIUM CEPA)

Planting: Start from sets for ease; can be started from seed as well. Plant sets in early spring, as soon as soil can be worked, as long as temperatures are over 30 degrees. Choose a site in full sun where onions won't be shaded. Use raised beds or rows 3 inches high, with loose, well-draining soil, where onions or garlic have not been grown the previous 2 years. Prepare beds with 3 inches of compost worked into the soil. Plant sets 1 inch deep, spaced 4 inches apart. If growing from seeds, plant in pots, pressing gently into soil with a chopstick and covering with plastic. If seedlings grow over 3 inches tall, cut back to aid transplanting. To transplant, wait until temperatures are consistently above 40 degrees.

Care: Hardy to Zone 3. Water 1 inch per week, more if it's dry, and use mulch to retain moisture and suffocate weeds. Sidedress with compost every 2 weeks until the bulbs appear. Do not cover exposed bulbs. Susceptible to thrips and onion maggots. If flowers appear, remove bulbs from garden, they're spent.

Harvesting: Harvest when onion tops yellow and fall over. Remove soil around bulbs for 2 days to encourage drying, then pull up and continue to dry for 2 weeks. Harvest before cool weather causes rot.

Seed saving: Requires pollination to set seeds. Allow onions to flower and for seeds to dry on the plant. When flower fades, bag heads to ensure seeds don't blow away.

Parsnips (Pastinaca sativa)

Planting: Use fresh seeds only; older seeds won't germinate. Direct sow in loamy, well-draining soil, that's loose and free of rocks, with a pH between 6.5 and 7. Before planting, add 2 inches of compost to the site. Wait until soil temperature is above 50 degrees, then sow seeds inch apart and cover with soil ½ an inch deep. Seedlings can take up to 30 days to appear. When 3 inches tall, thin first to 3 inches apart, then to 6 inches apart.

Care: Hardy to Zone 2. Needs full sun, but will tolerate some shade, especially in hot weather. Water 1 inch per week. Water during the summer if rainfall is less than 1 inch per week. Mulch to retain moisture and suppress weeds. Susceptible to aphids, leaf miners, and carrot rust flies.

Harvesting: Harvest when leaves die back, but before a hard freeze. Light freezes enhance flavor. If overwintering in the ground, cover with a thick layer of straw. Harvest as desired, but before new leaf growth the following spring.

Seed saving: Requires pollination so reserve several plants for seed saving to ensure viable seeds. Save seeds in the plant's second year. You will have to overwinter parsnips under 6 inches of straw in Northern climates. When flowers emerge, allow to turn brown and dry. Seed heads should ripen and dry on the plant. When dry, snip from plant and place in a plastic bag to complete drying process.

PEANUTS (ARACHIS HYPOGAEA)

Planting: Best if direct sown, but can be started indoors 8 weeks before the last spring frost date in Northern climates. If direct sowing, plant 3 weeks after the last spring frost date, when threat of frost has passed. Before planting, cultivate soil and amend with compost so peanuts can push through soil. Choose a site with loose, well-draining soil and full sun with a Southern exposure. Choose seed peanuts that are fresh, unroasted, and whole. Plant 2 inches deep and 10 inches apart. To start indoors, fill peat pots with soil and put 1 unroasted, fresh peanut in each pot, plant 1-inch deep. Transplant outside 10 inches apart when soil temperatures are at least 75 degrees F. Use black plastic if necessary to warm soil.

Care: Needs full sun and a Southern exposure. Water regularly. Hill plants when they reach 6 inches high. When yellow flowers appear and fade, plant will soon set peanuts.

Harvest: Requires 16 weeks to reach maturity. Harvest before fall frosts threaten by using a gardening fork. Let dry in a cool, dry area for 4 weeks.

Seed saving: Peanuts that have been harvested and properly dried can be planted the following summer.

Peas (Pisum sativum)

Planting: Direct sow 4 weeks before the last spring frost, when the soil temperature is at least 50 degrees, but before outside temperatures are consistently above 70. Choose a site in full sun, with rich, loamy, well-draining soil, with a pH of 7. Amend soil with bone meal or wood ashes before planting. Sow seeds 1 inch deep and 2 inches apart, in a site where peas weren't grown the previous year.

Care: Hardy to Zone 3. Needs full sun, but water sparingly, unless drought weather. Mulch to suppress weeds. Peas will fix nitrogen in the soil, making it available for other plants. Susceptible to aphids.

Harvesting: Pick every day or every other day to increase harvest. Pick peas mid-morning, after dew has evaporated. To harvest, snip pods from plant; don't pull. Peas are a nitrogen-fixer; plant heavy-nitrogen feeders at site after pea harvest.

Seed saving: Allow pods to fully mature and dry on plant. Once dry, snip pods from plant and remove peas. Harvest before rain threatens.

Peppers, Bell (Capsicum annuum)

Planting: Start seeds indoors 8 weeks before last spring frost date, or direct sow outside when soil temps are at least 70 degrees to encourage germination. Choose a site with loamy, well-draining soil, with a pH of 7. Before transplanting, amend soil with compost. Plant 18 inches apart, when outside temperatures are consistently above 65 degrees. Plant near wildflowers or bees to promote pollination.

Care: Hardy to Zone 3. Needs full sun, loves warm temperatures. Provide 1 inch of water a week, 2 inches each week when drought occurs. Mulch to retain moisture and suffocate weeds. Spray plants with 1 tablespoon Epsom salts mixed with 1 gallon of water when flowers appear, and side dress with compost when fruit sets. Susceptible to aphids, flea beetles, mosaic virus.

Harvesting: Harvest when peppers are desired size. To harvest, snip or gently cut peppers off plant.

Seed saving: Allow peppers to ripen well past edible stage and dry on plants. Bell peppers should be completely dry. Harvest by snipping pepper from plant, and gently opening pod. Remove seeds and allow to dry for another 2 weeks.

Potatoes (Solanum tuberosum)

Planting: Start with seed potatoes. Plant entire potato, or cut seed potatoes into 1-inch pieces, each with an "eye," and allow to heal for 24 hours after cutting. Plant 2 weeks after last spring frost date in loamy, well-draining soil with a pH between 5 and 5.2. Before planting, till compost into soil. Plant in trenches, sowing 12 inches apart and 4 inches deep, with the "eye" up.

Care: Hardy to Zone 3. Needs full sun and 1 inch of water each week, especially when tubers are forming. Start hilling dirt around plant when 6 inches tall, just before flowers bloom. Hill every couple of weeks. Susceptible to aphids, flea beetles, leafhoppers, early and late blight, and potato scab.

Harvesting: Harvest when plants start to fall over and die, usually after 12 weeks. Dig around plant, don't bruise or puncture potatoes. Gently brush off dirt, and allow to dry. Store in a cool place.

Seed saving: Use seed potatoes to propagate; saving seeds isn't necessary.

Radishes (Raphanus sativus)

Planting: Direct sow outdoors 4 weeks before the last spring frost date. Sow every 2 weeks for a continued harvest. Choose a site with fertile, well-draining soil in full sun, with a neutral pH, and where radishes haven't grown for 2 years. Sow seeds ½ inch deep and 1 inch apart. When sprouts emerge, thin to 2 inches. If planting in fall, start 8 weeks before first fall frost date, and plant every 2 weeks. Plant different varieties for interesting harvest.

Care: Hardy to Zone 2. Needs full sun, water 1 inch per week so roots don't get tough and woody. Thin to 2 inches; crowded radishes grow leaves but stunted roots.

Harvesting: Ready to harvest in 30 days. Harvest right away when ready, otherwise, roots will turn woody. To harvest, pull up, and brush off dirt.

Seed saving: Allow plant to flower and set seed pods. When blooms have faded, allow pods to dry completely on plant. Remove pods as soon as dry to ensure they don't split and drop seeds.

Spinach (Spinacia oleracea)

Planting: Start sowing outdoors when soil temperature is at least 40 degrees. Can survive light frost, needs 6 weeks of cool weather to grow well. Seeds won't germinate if soil temps are over 70 degrees. Choose a site with a pH of 7 and loamy, well-draining soil. Sow seeds by broadcasting and covering lightly with ½-inch of soil. Thin to 2 inches apart. Plant every 2 weeks to ensure a continual harvest. For fall harvest, plant 10 weeks before the first frost date, as long as temperatures are not too high. Plant next to radishes to deter pests.

Care: Hardy to Zone 3. Needs full sun, will tolerate part shade in the afternoons. Water regularly, keep soil moist with mulch. Susceptible to leaf miners, mosaic virus, and downy mildew.

Harvesting: Harvest when leaves are 4 to 6 inches; any larger, and they might be bitter.

Seed saving: Requires pollination to produce seeds. Allow plants to bolt, flower, and produce seeds. When female plants turn yellow, remove from garden. Place in paper bags and secure bags with a clip. Hang upside down until seeds drop.

SQUASH (CUCURBITA)

Types: Summer, Hubbard, Winter, Acorn, Butternut, Pumpkin, Zucchini, Decorative Gourds.

Planting: If starting inside, sow 4 weeks before your last spring frost date. If direct sowing, start outside when soil temps are at least 65 degrees, and threat of frost has passed. Cover with cold frames if temperatures dip below 65 degrees. Plant seeds 1 inch deep and 24 inches apart, in a site with loamy, well-draining soil. In warmer climates, plant a 2nd crop in late spring to avoid vine borers. Before planting, work 3 inches of compost into site. Plant near wildflowers or a beehive to promote pollination; if no insects are present or fruit is stunted, hand pollinate.

Care: Needs at least 8 hours of sun daily; in warm, dry climates, some afternoon shade is ok. Water at least 1 inch per week, more during dry spells. Mulch well to keep moist and stifle weeds. Side dress with compost when flowers appear, apply every 2 weeks until harvest ends. Susceptible to squash bugs, vine borers, cucumber beetle, blossom end rot, and aphids.

Harvesting: Harvest your summer squashes when they are the desired size, usually 60 days after transplanting. Check plants daily. Larger squashes can be tough; small squashes are more tender. Harvest winter squashes when rind is hard. To harvest, cut squashes off vine with a sharp knife. Pull plants up at the end of season and compost disease-free plants.

Seed saving: Harvest when skins are hard and dry. Carefully cut and remove seeds. Place seeds in a bowl of room-temperature water. Allow to ferment for 3 days to remove outer coat and cucumber pulp. After 3 days, separate seeds from water. Toss seeds that float; they're not viable. Spread viable seeds on paper towels and dry thoroughly.

Sunchokes (Helianthus tuberosus)

Planting: Plant from seed tubers from a friend, or order online. Can plant whole tuber or cut into pieces, each with a bud. If cutting, plant immediately. Choose a site in full sun, with pH of 6.5 to 7. Will grow in poor soil, but benefits from a well-composted site. Plant tubers 4 inches deep and 12 inches apart. If tubers have shoots, point upwards when planting.

Care: Hardy to Zone 4. Needs full sun and consistent watering to prevent woody tubers. Cut flower stalks to 4 feet tall to encourage tuber growth and discourage flowering. Side dress with compost mid-summer.

Harvesting: Harvest after first frost, when plants start to die. To harvest, dig around tubers and lift up. Can be left in the ground until needed. Mulch well to prevent freezing.

Seed saving: Requires tubers for propagation.

Sweet Potatoes (Ipomoea batatas)

Planting: Grown from slips. Either purchase or grow your own by allowing mature sweet potatoes to sprout. If sprouting your own, when slips are 5 inches tall, carefully remove and place in water. When slip root systems are well established, transfer to pots. When plants are established in pots, transplant outside. One sweet potato can yield up to 10 slips. Plant after the last spring frost date when temperatures are consistently over 70 degrees. Choose a site in full sun, with loamy, well-draining soil, and a neutral pH. Can grow in rows; hills in full sun are another option. Space slips 12 apart, and water generously to help roots establish.

Care: Hardy to Zone 7. Needs full sun, loves heat. Side dress with compost 30 days after transplanting. Water well, especially during dry weather. Provide lots of space; vines will grow rapidly. Susceptible to flea beetles and fungal leaf rot.

Harvesting: Start harvesting as early as 90 days after transplanting but wait until leaves turn yellow. Can wait until late fall, but harvest before frost threatens. To harvest, lift dirt with a garden fork; alternatively, follow each vine. When vines are difficult to pull up, check dirt for tubers. After harvest, cure sweet potatoes for 10 days before storing.

Seed saving: Propagate with slips.

Tomatoes (Lycopersicon esculentum)

Planting: Start seeds indoors 8 weeks before your last spring frost date. Plant in pots by putting 1 or 2 seeds in pots and covering with ½ inch of dirt. Seedlings should emerge within 14 days. Transplant when soil temps are at 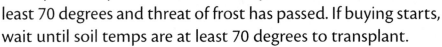 least 70 degrees and threat of frost has passed. If buying starts, wait until soil temps are at least 70 degrees to transplant.

Select a site with at least 6 hours of sun, and loamy, well-draining soil, with a pH between 5 and 6. Before transplanting, till 3 inches of compost into the site, and establish tomato cages at the time of planting. Space transplants 24 inches apart, planting deeply, and leaving 1 inch of plant above soil to promote good root growth.

Care: Hardy to Zone 3. Needs full sun. In Northern gardens make sure plants receive at least 6 hours of sun. Afternoon shade in warm climates promotes healthy growth. Provide 2 inches of water consistently each week. Mulch well to retain moisture. Side dress with compost when flowers appear. Pinch of suckers as they appear to promote fruit growth. Susceptible to aphids, mosaic virus, flea beetles, tomato hornworm, whiteflies, and blossom end rot.

Harvesting: Harvest when tomatoes are uniformly red and ready to drop off plant. If birds are an issue, harvest when tomatoes are green, place in a paper bag indoors to ripen. If a hard frost threatens, harvest all tomatoes.

Seed saving: Allow tomatoes to fully ripen on vine. Carefully cut and remove seeds and pulp. Place seeds in a bowl of room-temperature water. Allow to ferment for 3 days to remove outer coat and cucumber pulp. After 3 days, separate seeds from water. Toss seeds that float; they're not viable. Spread viable seeds on paper towels and dry thoroughly.

TURNIPS (BRASSICA RAPA)

Planting: Plant as soon as soil can be worked in spring. Choose a site in full sun, with loamy, well-draining soil, with a pH between 6.5 and 7. Before planting, work 2 inches of compost in and loosen soil to a 12-inch depth. To direct sow, broadcast seed, and cover with ½ inch of soil. When seedlings are 3 inches tall, thin to 4 inches apart for roots, 1 inch apart if grown for greens.

Care: Hardy to Zone 2. Needs full sun. Water 1 inch per week, mulch when plants are 3 inches high to retain moisture and suppress weeds. Susceptible to root maggots, aphids, flea beetles, and powdery mildew.

Harvesting: For greens, harvest when desired size. For roots, harvest up to 10 weeks; smaller roots are more tender. Overly mature roots can be woody. To harvest, pull up plant, or loosen soil and lift up.

Seed saving: Allow plant to bolt and set flowers. When blooms have faded, allow seeds to dry on stalk. When seeds are dry, pull plant and hang upside down to continue drying, making sure to bag the blooms to catch falling seeds.

ZUCCHINI (CUCURBITA PEPO VAR. CYLINDRICA)

❑ See Squash.

Chapter 10: Fruits of Your Labor

STRAWBERRIES (FRAGARIA)

Day-Neutral: Will produce berries regardless of day length as long as temperatures remain between 35 and 85 degrees.

Everbearer: Will produce berries continuously through summer and autumn. Produce fewer runners than June-bearing varieties, so multiple crops are possible. Two popular varieties are Seascape and Ozark Beauty.

Junebearer: June-bearing varieties produce fruit in one large crop over 10 to 14 days. Sensitive to day length.

For an extensive list of varieties by state, region, or province, visit http://strawberryplants.org/2010/10/strawberry-varieties-by-state/.

Planting: Plant as soon as the ground can be worked and last threat of frost has passed. Zones 3 through 6, plant in spring so they develop a strong root structure by winter. Zones 7 through 11, plant in fall to ensure a spring harvest. Best to buy starts for best results.

Space plants 12 to 18 inches apart, and make holes wide enough for 4 inch roots; trim roots if longer than 4 inches. Leave crown above the soil surface, otherwise the plant could rot. Plant in full sun. Prefers loamy, well-draining soil with pH between 5.5 and 7. Amend heavy soil (like clay) with composted leaves to lighten soil before transplanting. Improve dry, sandy soil with compost. Plant near wildflowers or a beehive since strawberries require pollination to develop fruit. Don't plant in a site that had strawberries, tomatoes, peppers, or eggplants the previous year.

Care: Needs at least 8 hours of sun daily and 1 inch of water per per week, especially, during heat and drought. Mulch to keep soil moist and berries clean. Cover plants with bird netting to protect berries. Susceptible to powdery mildew, leaf blight, Japanese beetles, spider mites, and slugs. Clip off all but 3 runners in fall to improve harvest the following spring.

Harvesting: Berries ripen 30 days after pollination. Harvest only red berries and pick every 3 days by cutting the stem with scissors.

Raspberries (Rubus)

Summer-bearer: Produces a single crop in summertime on 2nd year canes.

Ever-bearer: Produces two crops, one in summer and one in fall.

Fall-fruiting[4]: Produces one crop in late summer and fall on the current year canes.

Planting: Plant in early spring in cool climates, late winter in warmer areas. Establish a trellis before planting to avoid disturbing roots. Prefers a soil pH between 5.5 and 7. Soak roots for 1 hour before transplanting to reduce shock. Space plants about 3 feet apart, in rows 8 feet apart so roots can spread. After transplanting, cut back canes to 8 inches. Don't plant near wild-growing berries to avoid diseases and pests.

Care: Hardy to Zone 2. Mulch deeply to conserve moisture. Water one inch per week. Side-dress with compost in early spring. Prune back dead or dying canes in the fall to ensure a bigger harvest next year. Prune during summer if plants become unruly. Susceptible to powdery mildew and cane borers.

Harvesting: Will ripen over 10 to 14 days. Pick berries every couple of days after dew has evaporated.

BLACKBERRIES (RUBUS FRUTICOSUS)

Training: Produces berries in 2nd year. Not cold hardy.

Erect: Produces berries in 2nd year. Need to be pruned consistently.

Primocane-fruiting: Produces fruit on first year canes. Prune canes to the ground each winter for best results.

Semi-erect: Thornless. Produces fruit on first year canes. Higher yield than other types.

Planting: Plant in early spring in full sun and in well-draining, slightly acidic soil. Amend site with compost for nutrients and

2 tablespoons vinegar to a gallon of water for acidity. Add trellis before planting to preserve roots. Space plants 5 to 6 feet apart in rows 8 feet apart.

Care: Hardy to Zone 5, but cover in early spring if chance of frost. Requires full sun. Self-fertile, don't plant near wild varieties to avoid disease and pests. Prune back all canes in winter.

Harvesting: Pick berries every other day when ripe. Pick with the central plug (white part) intact.

BLUEBERRIES (VACCINIUM)

Highbush: Hardy to Zone 4. Native to eastern United States. Can grow 5 to 8 feet high.

Lowbush: Hardy to Zone 3. Shorter than highbush varieties, topping out under 18 inches.

Planting: Start with plants at least 1 year old. Loves acidic soil, so amend planting site with 2 tablespoons vinegar in 1 gallon of water so soil pH is between 4 and 5. Space bushes 5 feet apart.

Care: Hardy to Zone 3. Requires full sun and consistent watering of 1 inch per week, 2 inches during dry spells. Mulch deeply to maintain moisture so shallow root system doesn't dry out. Pinch blooms in first and second year to promote plant growth. Avoid pruning until winter of fourth year, when pruning is necessary to encourage higher yields. Self-fertile so avoid planting next to wild berries. Susceptible to powdery mildew.

Harvesting: Pick fruit in late summer starting plant's 3rd year. Production highest in 6th year. Wait until berries fall into your hands to harvest for best results.

BOYSENBERRY (RUBUS URSINUS X RUBUS IDAEUS)

Planting: Raspberry, blackberry, and loganberry hybrid. Thornless varieties bear less fruit, but are easier to harvest. Plant canes in loamy, well-drained soil, about 4 to 5 feet apart.

Care: Hardy to Zone 4. Needs full sun and regular waterings. Prune old growth after second year, since berries grow on one-year-old canes. Leave any new canes alone when pruning. They will fruit next year. Use mesh to protect berries from birds.

Harvest: Berries are ripe when they have turned dark red or black color in July or August. Similar to blackberries, the white plug should come off the plant along when harvested.

LOGANBERRY (RUBUS X LOGANOBACCUS)

Planting: Hybrid of raspberry and a blackberry varieties. Before planting, add compost to soil and establish a vertical trellis. Plant canes in late fall or early spring, 4 feet apart, in well-draining, loamy soil out of the wind, and that gets full sun.

Care: Needs full sun, but will tolerate some shade in the afternoon. Water regularly, feed with compost every spring. Doesn't do well on horizontal trellis; train to vertical trellis. Berries grow on year-old canes, so start pruning in second year. After harvest, cut spent canes down to ground level, leaving new growth alone. Susceptible to raspberry leaf spot fungus and dryberry.

Harvest: When ripe, berries will turn a deep red or purple in mid to late summer, and can last for 60 days. Pick daily for best harvest; berries ripen at various times. Wear gloves and long sleeves since vines will be thorny.

Currants *(Ribes)*

Types: Black, red, & white

Planting: Choose 1 or 2 year old plants, and select a site that's cool with good air circulation and partial shade. Fertile, well-draining soil with a pH around 6.5 is best. Work compost into the site prior to planting. Plant early fall or late winter, spaced 5 feet apart.

Care: Hardy to Zone 3. Water well and keep cool. Mulch well. Pinch off any flowers in the first year to allow roots to establish. After first year, prune back, allowing 8 or so branches to remain. In second year, prune back most 2-year-old growth, leaving 3 or 4 canes and 4 to 5 one-year-old canes. In third year of growth, prune all except 3 or 4 canes of each year. In fourth year, remove all 4-year-old canes, allowing new growth to remain, as well as 2- and 3-year-old growth. Following this strategy leads to better harvests.[5] Remove diseased canes or canes that lay on the ground of any age. Prune in late winter when plants are dormant. Susceptible to white pine blister rust.

Harvest: Ready to harvest when berries are appropriate color for their type in June. Lasts 2 weeks. Full harvests occur in 3rd year and every year after.

Gooseberries (Ribes uva-crispa)

Plant: Plant bushes 2 or 3 years old in late autumn or early spring. Plant in full sun, in loamy, well-draining soil, 4 to 5 feet apart.

Care: Keep watered and in full sun. Feed with compost every spring, and mulch well to keep moist. Protect berries from birds with netting. Susceptible to the gooseberry sawfly and gooseberry mildew.

Harvest: Green, under-ripe berries good for jams and pies, ready to harvest in early summer. Harvest red berries mid-summer.

Grapes (*Vitis*)

Red and white table: Varieties appropriate for eating. Not suitable for wines.

Red and white wine: Suitable for making wines. Varieties depend on region, soil type.

For a full list of varieties, visit https://en.wikipedia.org/wiki/List_of_grape_varieties

Planting: Plant vines in their first year, but before planting, install a trellis and soak roots in water for 2 hours to aid transplanting. Prefers soil in full sun with a pH of 5.8 to 7, and needs loose soil that drains well. Plant 6 feet apart, in holes 12 inches deep and 12 inches wide. Most grape varieties are self-fertile, but double check before selecting varieties.

Care: Hardy to Zone 2. Provide full sun and good air circulation. Don't allow fruiting until the vine's third year to establish good root growth. Prune vigorously in early spring; canes only produce fruit once. Side dress with compost lightly in second year of growth. Mulch to retain moisture. Susceptible to powdery mildew, birds, japanese beetles, and aphids. Use bird netting to protect fruit.

Harvesting: Ready to harvest when grapes are fully colored, plump, and easily crushed. Will not ripen off the vine, so wait until you're sure they're ripe.

Figs (Ficus carica)

Types: More than 200 fig varieties exist. Popular varieties are Brown Turkey, Chicago, and Celeste.

Planting: If you live in a cold zone, it's best to grow figs in containers. Make sure the variety you choose is self-pollinating. After transitioning to a pot, feed with a layer of compost.

Care: Cold hardy to Zone 8. Water regularly, especially when water is dry an inch below surface. Mulch deeply, and feed monthly during the growing season. Bring indoors for winter, plant will drop leaves and go dormant. Keep watering throughout dormancy, and move outside when weather is warm again. Susceptible to aphids.

Harvesting: In Zones 8 to 11, harvest in June and late summer/early fall. In Zones 3 to 7, will ripen in June only. Harvest often. Fruit will be soft and may split.

Part 3: The Organic Rebel's Plant Encyclopedia & Growing Guide

Popular raspberry varieties:

Black	Purple	Gold, autumn fruiting	Red, autumn fruiting	Red, late summer	Red, mid-summer	Red, early summer
Black Hawk	Brandywine	Anne	Amity	Cascade Delight	Cuthbert	Boyne
Bristol	Glencoe	Fallgold	Augusta	Coho	Lloyd George	Fertödi Venus
Cumberland	Royalty	Fertödi Aranyfürt	Joan J. (Thornless)	Fertödi Rubina	Meeker	Rubin Bulgarski
Jewel		Goldenwest	Caroline	Octavia	Newburgh	Cascade Dawn
Munger		Golden Queen	Zeva Herbsternte	Schoenemann	Ripley	Glen Clova
Ohio Everbearer		Honey Queen	Heritage	Tulameen	Skeena	Killarney
Scepter		Kiwi Gold	Josephine		Cowichan	Malahat
			Ripley		Chemainus	Malling Exploit
			Summit		Saanich	Titan
						Willamette

Chapter 11: Herb Delight

ANISE (PIMPINELLA ANISUM)

Purpose: Culinary

Planting: Will reach 18 to 24 inches. Sow seeds in full sun when soil temperature is 70 degrees or more. Direct sow since plant doesn't transplant well. Cover seeds with a dusting of soil. Keep moist, and expect seedlings in approximately a week.

Care: Water when dry, preferably early morning or late afternoon.

Harvesting: When seeds appear, snip flower stalk, and hang upside down. Cover the flower with a paper bag.

BASIL (OCIMUM BASILICUM)

Purpose: Culinary, medicinal

Planting: Start seeds indoors 6 weeks before the last spring frost. Soil should be around 70 degrees F for best growth.

Needs 6 to 8 hours of sun daily. Transplant 12 to 24 inches apart after the last frost date.

Care: Water plants consistently, and keep soil moist. Pinch flower heads as soon as they appear so leaves continue growing.

Harvesting: Pick leaves regularly to encourage continual growth. Harvest right before flowers bloom for best results.

Bay (Laurus nobilis)

Purpose: Culinary

Planting: Bay leaf trees are usually propagated by cuttings, so you will have to find a friend who has one or buy some of the internet (http://thefrugalchicken.com/bay). Root cuttings in water, then transfer to a pot.

Care: Hardy to USDA plant hardiness zone 7, and susceptible to frost. Provide full sun with a Southern exposure. Move indoors if there's a chance of frost. Grows best in temperatures between 45 to 64 degrees F.

Harvesting: Harvest mature leaves for the best flavor.

Chamomile, German (Matricaria recutita)

Purpose: Teas, medicinal

Planting: Direct sow in late summer by broadcasting, then scratching into the soil. Germination in 1 to 2 weeks. Grows best in full sun, and in slightly acidic soil. Space plants 6 inches apart. Will tolerate some

Roman Chamomile

shade. Plant near wheat, onions, cabbage, and cucumbers. Increases the essential oil production other herbs nearby.

Care: Will grow in less than ideal soil. Once established, is very hardy. Susceptible to aphids and mealy bug, known to attract bees, butterflies.

Harvesting: Harvest flowers daily in the morning before the sun gets hot. Dry before using as a tea.

Chamomile, Roman (Anthemis nobilis)

Purpose: Teas, medicinal

Planting: Prefers cool temperatures, and can tolerate a light frost. Start seed indoors 6 weeks before the last spring frost or when soil is 70 degrees. Seedlings will emerge in 2 to 3 weeks.

Care: Hardy to USDA Zone 4. Needs full sun. Water well, providing 1 inch of water or rain per week.

Harvesting: Flowers less than German Chamomile. Harvest flowers daily in the morning before the sun gets hot. Dry before using as a tea.

Catnip (Nepeta cataria)

Purpose: Medicinal

Planting: A member of the mint family, grows well in most soils. Does best in well-draining, loamy soil. Direct sow late fall or early spring. Broadcast and scratch seeds into soil. Space plants 12 to 18 inches apart. Seedlings emerge in in 7 to 10 days.

Care: Grows best in full sun, but will tolerate some shade. Water regularly. Hardy to Zone 3. As it grows, pinch off the tops of stems to encourage bushy growth.

Harvesting: Harvest after established, however essential oils are at peak when the plant flowers. Harvest leaves and flowers mid-day to avoid mold during drying. Cut stems at the base of plant to aid drying.

Chervil (Anthriscus cerefolium)

Purpose: Culinary

Planting: Hardy to Zone 2. Direct sow seeds by broadcasting and scratching into the soil. Thin to 9 inches apart in an area that gets part shade to deter bolting in summer. Chervil develops a long, delicate taproot, so transplanting can trigger bolting. Plant near lettuce, cabbage, and kale to enhance flavor and for shade.

Care: Keep in part shade and water regularly so soil stays damp and cool. Grows well in any soil, although loamy soil is best. Cover with a cold frame to overwinter. Helps repel slugs and snails.

Harvesting: Start harvesting when plants are 4' tall.

Chives (Allium schoenoprasum)

Purpose: Culinary

Planting: Direct sow in rich, loamy soil that's well-draining and gets full sun. Till in 4 inches of compost in the garden site before planting. Sow when soil is 70 degrees F.

Care: Water consistently and keep soil moist for best results. Keep in full sun and protect in cool weather with a cold frame. Side dress with compost 60 days after sowing.

Harvesting: Start harvesting 60 days after sowing by trimming, but leaving some to continue growing.

DILL (ANETHUM GRAVEOLENS)

Purpose: Culinary

Dill

Planting: Dill does not transplant well, so direct sow dill seeds by broadcasting in rich, loamy soil and scratching into the earth when soil is at least 70 degrees. Prefers full sun. After 10 to 14 days, seedlings should appear. Thin to 18 inches apart. Sow every 2 weeks for a continual harvest. Plant near cabbage.

Care: Shelter plants from winds, and water well. Pinch off flowers to extend your harvest. Dill attracts beneficial insects to your garden. Keep away from carrots for best results.

Harvesting: Start harvesting when 5 or more leaves appear. To harvest, snip leaves with scissors, leaving the rest of the plant intact for a continual harvest.

FENNEL (FOENICULUM VULGARE)

Purpose: Culinary

Planting: Direct sow or transplant after the last spring frost in loamy soil that drains well. Needs full sun for best results.

Work rich compost into soil before planting. Seedlings should appear in 7 to 10 days. Thin to 6 inches apart.

Care: Keep soil consistently moist. Requires at an inch of water each week, more during hotter months. Keep in full sun. Pinch off flowers for continued harvest. Will tolerate light frost under a row cover.

Harvesting: Ready to harvest after 90 days. To harvest, trim leaves but don't over trim. As you harvest, the plant will become bushier. Harvest bulbs once they 4 inches across.

Feverfew (Tanacetum parthenium)

Purpose: Medicinal

Planting: Direct sow in early spring when soil reaches 60 degrees. Needs full sun and loamy soil with good drainage. Broadcast seeds and tamp down. Seeds need sunlight to germinate, so don't cover with soil. Water gently, and seedlings should appear in 10 to 14 days. When the plants are 6 inches tall, thin to 10 inches apart.

Care: Keep in full sun. Water well, but do not overwater. Well-rooted mature plants are cold hardy down to -20 degrees F in a coldframe. Susceptible to aphids, leaf miners, and chrysanthemum nematodes.

Harvesting: Harvest for medicinal use when flowers are in full bloom, but plant still has plenty of leaves and hasn't gone to seed. Pinch off flowers and dry.

Garlic (Allium sativum)

Purpose: Culinary and medicinal

Planting: Separate bulbs into cloves and plant 2 inches deep and 4 inches apart in well-drained, loamy soil in full sun. Prefers slightly acidic to neutral soil. Plant in the spring as soon soil is workable or in fall 6 to 8 weeks before first frost date. To plant, place the root end down and pointed end facing up to the sky. If planting in the fall, shoots will appear as weather warms.

Care: Cold hardy to Zone 3 and frost tolerant when mulched heavily with straw. Remove mulch in the spring after last frost date to promote bulbing. Pinch off flowers to promote good bulb growth. Side dress with compost if leaves start to yellow prematurely. Be sue to water consistently during bulbing, but don't overwater to preserve husks.

Harvesting: Harvest garlic when tops yellow and fall over. Check 1 one 2 bulbs; if cloves haven't formed, leave alone for 7 to 10 days before checking again. To harvest, dig around bulb and carefully lift out with a hand trowel or garden fork. Carefully brush off soil, keeping papery skins intact, and cure on a shady porch for two weeks.

Horehound (Marrubium vulgare)

Purpose: Teas, medicinal, candy

Planting: Seed germination is spotty; best to use transplants or cuttings. If seeding, broadcast and scratch into earth; keep moist until seedlings appear. Thin to 10 to 12 inches apart.

Plant near tomatoes and peppers to improve fruiting. Plant in an area that gets full sun.

Care: Hardy to USDA Zone 4. Requires full sun. Grows well in infertile, dry soils. Water sparingly, but side dress with compost to encourage growth. Attracts beneficial insects.

Harvesting: Harvest leaves for candy or medicinal use when the plant flowers.

Hyssop (Hyssopus officinalis)

Purpose: Medicinal

Planting: Start indoors 8 weeks before last spring front. Can direct sow in warmer zones. When starting by direct sowing, broadcast over earth, and scratch gently into soil. If starting indoors, cover with a thin layer of soil. Seedlings emerge in 2 to 3 weeks. Thin to or transplant 8 inches apart. Hyssop prefers rocky, well-draining soil.

Care: Requires full sunlight, but is tolerant of shade part of the day. Prefers heat and dryer conditions. Water but don't overwater. Hardy to USDA Zone 3. Attracts bees, repels flea beetles and cabbage moths.

Harvesting: Harvest leaves once flowering begins. Snip with scissors and dry. To harvest seeds, let the seed pods dry out completely then snip. Will self-seed.

Lavender (Lavandula)

Purpose: Scent, culinary, medicinal

Planting: Starting with transplants is best. Seeds are slow to germinate, requiring a chilling period of about 4 weeks. Start seeds indoors in pots 12 weeks before your last spring frost date, and place pots covered with plastic in a cool area at about 40 degrees. After chilling period, remove to a warmer area, and seedlings should emerge quickly. When 6 inches tall, transplant into well-drained, slightly alkaline soil 12 inches apart.

Care: Prefers areas with full sun, Southern exposure, and good circulation. Needs 1 inch of rainfall or watering each week. Hardy to USDA Zone 5, but won't tolerate frost. When temperatures dip, use a row cover.

Harvesting: Harvest when flowers emerge. Trim flowers to encourage continued blooming into fall.

Lemon Balm (Melissa officinalis)

Purpose: Culinary, teas, medicinal

Planting: Starting with transplants is easiest, but can be started by seed indoors 6 weeks before the last frost date or outside by broadcasting and scratching into soil in late spring/early summer. Grow in full sun, in well-drained clay or loamy soil with a pH range of 6 to 7.5. Seedlings will emerge in 2 to 3 weeks. Will tolerate some shade. Transplant or thin to 12 inches apart. Does well in pots.

Care: Hardy to Zone 4. Water well, use mulch to prevent drying out. Avoid watering leaves to prevent mildew. Side dress with compost.

Harvesting: Harvest leaves anytime after plant is established

Lemon Verbena (Aloysia citrodora)

Purpose: Scent, teas, culinary

Planting: Best when started with cuttings. Gather cuttings in late spring, when plant is still in dormancy. Encourage root growth by placing cuttings in a mason jar of water. Once the plant has a good root structure, transplant 12 inches apart to a container or outdoors to full sun and fertile soil.

Care: Grows best in full sun, but will tolerate some afternoon shade. Not frost tolerant, so use row covers or grow in pots to move indoors. Side dress with compost when transplanted, or every 2 weeks if grown in pots.

Harvesting: Harvest leaves when the plant is established.

Lovage (Levisticum officinale)

Purpose: Culinary

Planting: Direct sow outdoors by broadcasting, then covering lightly with dirt when soil temps are at least 60 degrees. Sow indoors 6 weeks before the last frost date. Prefers loamy soil with a pH of 6.5. Transplant 8 inches apart. Plant near potatoes, sweet potatoes, and root crops.

Care: Hardy to Zone 4. Best grown in full sun. Water regularly.

Harvesting: Harvest leaves when plant is well established in late summer. To harvest roots, dig up in the fall, leaving some for next season.

Marjoram (Origanum majorana)

Purpose: Culinary

Planting: Direct sow outside in fall or in very early spring in a cold frame. Prefers soil pH between 6.5 and 7, but will grow in slightly acidic or alkaline soil. If starting inside, sow 6 weeks before your last frost date. Seeds germinate in 2 weeks. Transplant outside 18 inches apart in loamy soil with compost worked in. Also propagates well with cuttings or root ball division. Requires full sun.

Care: Hardy to Zone 6. Water regularly, but don't overwater. Keep in full sun, side dress with compost mid-summer. Cover in a cold frame to protect from frost and extend your growing season. Susceptible to whitefly and thrips.

Harvesting: Harvest late spring into fall by snipping leaves and stems as needed.

Mint (Mentha)

Purpose: Culinary, scent, teas, medicinal

Planting: Will grow from seed, but easier to establish from cuttings. If growing from seed, sow indoors 8 weeks before the last spring frost date. Germinate in soil 70 degrees or higher. Seedlings emerge in 1 to 2 weeks. Plant outside in early spring in full sun. Will grow in most soil types, but does best in loamy soil with good drainage. Will tolerate some shade. Plant 24 inches apart in moist soil. Plant near cabbage and tomatoes to improve flavor.

Care: Protect young transplants from wind and direct sun for long periods. Use mulch to keep moist, and side dress plants with compost once a month. In fall, protect from frost with a cold frame winter protection in cold climates. Susceptible to powdery mildew and leaf spot.

Harvesting: Harvest frequently as soon as transplants are well established, or when established plants emerge in spring.

OREGANO (ORIGANUM VULGARE)

Purpose: Culinary, medicinal

Planting: Can propagate by seed or cuttings. Sow seeds indoors 10 weeks before the last spring frost. Press into soil, mist with water, and cover with plastic. Direct sow outside after the last spring frost by broadcasting and scratching into the earth when soil is at least 70 degrees. Plant 8 inches apart, or thin to 8 inches apart. Does best in full sun and loamy, well-drained soil.

Care: Drought-tolerant, and only requires watering during very dry periods. Side dress with compost mid-season. Susceptible to aphids and spider mites

Harvesting: Harvest as needed when plants have reached 6 inches tall, but best flavor occurs as flower buds form. Harvest mid-morning, once dew has dried to avoid mold while preserving.

PARSLEY (PETROSELINUM CRISPUM)

Purpose: Culinary

Planting: Plant indoors 12 weeks before your last spring frost date. Soak the seeds overnight for faster germination. Likes cold weather, so direct sow outside 21 days before the last spring frost date. Seeds germinate in 21 to 30 days. Broadcast seeds about 6 inches apart when soil is at least 70 degrees. Soil should be loamy, moist, and fertile. Plant parsley in full sun next to asparagus, corn, and tomatoes to improve taste.

Care: Water evenly, especially when weather is warm. Dries out easily. Parsley is susceptible to black swallowtail larvae, carrot flies, and celery flies.

Harvesting: Harvest when leaves have 3 true segments. To harvest, snip outside leaves, keeping inner leaves intact so they can mature. Premature snipping will result in reduced harvest.

PENNYROYAL, AMERICAN (HEDEOMA PULEGIOIDES)

Purpose: Medicinal, scent, teas

Planting: Different than European Pennyroyal. Native to Eastern North America. Direct sow outside when threat of frost has passed by broadcasting and misting soil lightly. Sow indoors in pots by pressing seeds lightly into soil. Requires light to germinate, but grows quickly once seedlings emerge. Sprouting takes 14 to 21 days. Thin to or transplant 6 inches apart. Will grow in poor soil, but prefers pH of 6 to 7.5.

Care: Requires full sun, but will grow where other plants won't. Water, but don't overwater.

Harvesting: Harvest mid-summer as needed.

PENNYROYAL, EUROPEAN (MENTHA PULEGIUM)

Planting: Direct sow outside when threat of frost has passed by broadcasting and misting soil lightly. Sow indoors in pots by pressing seeds lightly into soil. Requires light to germinate, but grows quickly once seedlings emerge. Sprouting takes 14 to 21 days. Thin to or transplant 6 inches apart. Will grow in poor soil, but prefers pH of 6 to 7.5. Pregnant women should avoid contact.

Care: Hardy to Zone 5. Prefers full sun, will tolerate some shade. Hardy, will grow in poor soil, but does best in well-draining, loamy soil.

Harvest: Snip stems and leaves as needed. Harvest after plant is well-established and mid-morning, after dew has dried.

Rosemary (Rosmarinus officinalis)

Purpose: Culinary

Planting: Start from seed 12 weeks before last spring frost date. Use a heat mat to aid germination. Press seeds into soil, and cover with plastic wrap until seedlings emerge. Transplant into loamy soil, 12 inches apart, when night temperatures exceed 60 degrees. Prefers full sun, but will grow in part shade.

Care: Drought resistant, will grow in poor soil, but side dress with compost for best results. Water, but don't over water. Hardy to Zone 7, will not tolerate frost. Bring inside or cover if nighttime temperatures dip below 60 degrees.

Harvesting: Harvest leaves as needed when well established.

Rue (Ruta graveolens)

Purpose: Medicinal, culinary

Planting: Start from seed 8 weeks before last frost date. Requires light to germinate; press seeds into soil, cover with plastic, and position a grow light 1 inch above. Soil should be

70 degrees. Seedlings emerge in 7 to 30 days. Transplant to loamy, well-draining soil in full sun. Plant next to strawberries, figs, and raspberries.

Care: Hardy to Zone 4. Will thrive in dry conditions in full sun and poor soil. Cover when frost threatens. Mulch to overwinter. Keep away from basil, sage, and mint; rue will inhibit their growth.

Harvesting: Harvest leaves before rue flowers, otherwise leaves turn bitter. Harvest flowers in full bloom, but before seeds appear. Rue's essential oils can cause photodermatitis, so wear gloves when harvesting, especially if you have sensitive skin.

Sage (Salvia officinalis)

Purpose: Culinary, scent

Planting: Best to propagate from cuttings, but can be grown from seed. Start indoors 10 weeks before the last spring frost. When 3 inches tall, transplant outdoors 24 inches apart and 1 week before the last spring frost, or when soil temperatures are above 65 degrees. Water regularly until fully grown.

Care: Hardy to zone 5. Needs full sun, prefers loamy, well-draining soil. Side dress with compost when transplanted. Prune back any woody stems as the plant matures and at the start of every spring. Plant near rosemary, cabbage, and carrots. Keep away from cucumbers. Susceptible to powdery mildew, leaf spots, whiteflies, and aphids.

Harvesting: Harvest sage leaves mid-summer to fall, when plant is well established.

Savory (Satureja hortensis)

Purpose: Culinary

Planting: Start indoors 6 weeks before the last frost date. Needs light to germinate, so press seeds lightly into soil, and cover with plastic. Keep soil at 70 degrees or higher. Sprouts should emerge in 14 days. Transplant 10 inches apart. If direct sowing, broadcast seeds in well-draining soil after threat of frost has passed and soil is at least 70 degrees. Thin to 10 inches apart.

Care: Prefers full sun, and a soil pH around 7. Keep moist and side dress with compost when transplanting. For best results, add compost again mid-summer. Plant next to beans and tomatoes.

Harvesting: Harvest leaves when plant reaches 6 inches tall, in about 80 days. Harvest mid-morning after dew has dried to prevent mold.

Sorrel (Rumex acestosa)

Purpose: Culinary

Planting: Direct sow ½ inch deep and 3 inches apart, 2 weeks before the last spring frost date. Does best in loamy, well-draining soil in full sun. Thin to 12 inches apart when plants are 2 months old.

Care: Hardy to Zone 5. Cover if frost threatens and to extend growing season. Does best with a soil pH between 5.5 to 7. Keep evenly moist, and side dress with compost when seedlings emerge, reapply mid-season. Plant sorrel near strawberries. Susceptible to aphids.

Harvesting: Harvest young leaves when plants are 5 inches tall, but don't over harvest. Snip off flowers before they set seeds to continue harvest into the fall.

Tarragon, French (*Artemisia dracunculus*)

Purpose: Culinary

Planting: Won't grow from seeds, so take cuttings from an existing plant or purchase plants. Transplant in loamy, well-draining soil, 24 inches apart.

Care: Does best in full sun, but will tolerate some shade. Prefers soil with a pH around 7. Water, but don't overwater, otherwise roots can rot. Does best in areas where summers are not too hot or too humid. Prune to prevent overgrowth. Mulch in late fall to overwinter. Plant near tomatoes and peppers. Susceptible to downy mildew and powdery mildew.

Harvesting: Harvest regularly when well established to keep healthy and prevent overgrowth and disease.

THYME (THYMUS VULGARIS)

Purpose: Culinary

Planting: Start seeds indoors 10 weeks before last frost date. Germination is slow, and it's best to transplant from cuttings or buy starts. Transplant 10 inches apart, 2 weeks before the the last spring frost date or when soil is at least 70 degrees.

Care: Hardy to Zone 5. Water well, especially during dry spells. Prefers well-drained soil and full sun, but will tolerate some shade. In fall, mulch plants to protect roots from freezes. Plant next tomatoes and cabbage.

Harvesting: Snip stems as desired after plant is well established.

Part 4: Nurturing Your Garden Organic Rebel Style

Chapter 12: Composting Guerillas

We all know composting equals a better gardening and in this chapter, you'll learn now to make your own compost. Composting involves recycling of natural matter like vegetable peels, coffee grounds, animal manure, grass clippings, leaves, and eggshells to make a healthy, nutritious fertilizer for your growing plants. In this chapter, we'll cover several types of composting, including an option if you can't have a compost pile in your backyard.

COLD COMPOSTING

By far, the simplest way to make a compost pile is to toss your kitchen scraps and yard waste into a pile and wait for it to rot. This is called cold composting, and it's a perfectly acceptable method, and one many people choose. Simply layer your kitchen waste and when all that's left is black dirt, you're ready to use it in your garden. If you have enough room, it's worth having 2-3 compost piles going at a time. At least one pile will be fully composted while the other pile is just beginning.

Hot composting

Four ingredients are required to make hot compost: nitrogen, carbon, air, and water. Together, these items feed microorganisms, and the proper ratio speeds up the process of decay. The rate that the organic material in your compost pile decomposes is dependent on the ratio of carbon-rich matters (called BROWN MATTER because it's dry, hence brown) and nitrogen-rich matter (called GREEN MATTER because it's fresh and moist).

The trick to successful compost is balancing ingredients high in nitrogen, such as fresh grass clippings, weeds, and kitchen scraps, with those high in carbon, dry leaves, straw, dried grass, sticks, and eggshells. Too much nitrogen causes an anaerobic compost pile while too much carbon results in compost that never heats to a high enough temperature to kill microbes.

According to Cornell University[3], the ideal ratio of green matter to brown for a compost pile is 1 to 30. The simplest way to apply this ratio in your hot compost pile is to include 2 parts of green material (e.g., fresh kitchen scraps) to one part brown material (e.g., dried leaves) to your pile.

When creating your compost pile, alternative layers of nitrogen and carbon matter. You can also incorporate horse, cow, rabbit, chicken, or pig manure. Once your layers are created, lightly water the pile so it's evenly moist. Too much water will interfere with aeration; too little water and the pile won't ferment.

After 3 to 4 weeks, the pile will have shrunk in size; this is normal. When the internal temperature has reached 130-150 degrees, dig into the pile with a spading fork and completely turn it over until the contents are redistributed. Let the pile rest so the temperature will rise again. When your pile has turned into black dirt, it's fully composted.

What's green composting material & what's brown?

In this chart, you'll find an easy reference for both green and brown compost material.

Brown	Green
Leaves	Animal manure*
Straw or Hay	Kitchen scraps
Sawdust	Coffee Grounds
Dried Twigs/Pine Needles	Fresh yard/garden waste
Wood chips	Fresh green woods
Paper/Newspaper	Seaweed

*Do not use cat, dog, or human manure

Building a compost bin

You can build a simple composting bin with recycled heat-treated pallets (if they're heat treated, they're safe to reuse). Nail each pallet to a 5 foot tall fence post or 4x4 posts, creating a 3-sided compost bin. You can start adding your kitchen, garden, and yard waste immediately.

CREATING COMPOST IN YOUR KITCHEN WITH RED WRIGGLERS

This is a fun activity if you want to create compost for your garden but don't have room for or aren't allowed to have a compost pile. We enjoyed doing this in our condo before we got our homestead. You can get healthy red wiggler worms (*Eisenia fetida*) from friends, or you can buy them online http://thefrugalchicken.com/worms.

You will also need two containers for your worms. We used food-safe plastic bins. The idea is the worms eat kitchen scraps in one bin. When the first bin is full of healthy compost and worm castings, you allow them to travel to the second bin (positioned below the first bin) using holes you drilled into the bottom of each bin. The process then starts over again as you use the compost in your garden.

HOW TO BUILD A WORM COMPOSTING BIN

TOOLS NEEDED:

- ❑ 2 small food-safe plastic bins with lids
- ❑ Drill with ¼-inch bit
- ❑ Newspaper torn into strips
- ❑ A handful of soil
- ❑ Kitchen scraps
- ❑ Red wrigglers

First, drill several holes on the bottom of each bin. Next, layer strips of newspaper lightly until the bins are full. Toss a handful of dirt into one of the bins, as well as kitchen scraps. Finally, place your worms in the bin. They will naturally start gravitating towards the food, consume it, and leave healthy castings and compost for you to use in your garden. Replace the kitchen scraps every few days or when your worms have eaten them all. Don't use dairy or meat products in your worm bin; stick to vegetable, fruit, and egg kitchen scraps.

Chapter 13: Water, Water Everywhere

When it comes to your garden, the amount of care you give it will dictate how well your vegetables grow. Plants need water to survive and grow, but their requirements vary depending on the weather, the soil quality, and the plant type, age, and size.

While you can use county or town water to give your garden a drink, if you object to using treated water, an alternative is collecting rainwater in barrels. In Chapter 16: Self-Sufficient Water With Rain Barrels, you'll find an in depth discussion about how to choose, install, and use rain barrels.

As a general rule of thumb, one inch of rain or supplemental water each week will keep most vegetable plants in your garden healthy. Water early in the day or in the evening to minimize evaporation and to avoid sunburning your leaves during the hottest days of summer. Check soil for moisture by poking a finger into it; if soil feels dry 1 inch down, it's time to water.

THE 6 COMMANDMENTS OF WATERING

Thou shalt keep the soil in your garden evenly moist: Plants that are starved of water one week then drowned the next week are more likely to have issues with diseases, split fruit, or weak roots. Keep the soil evenly moist so your plants have a consistent water supply.

Thou shalt allow the soil to dry out slightly when your plants are in the seedling stage to promote good root growth: While you don't want your plants to get thirsty, encourage healthy root growth by letting the soil dry out slightly before watering. This is a tactic only used as the plant is growing, not when it's flowering or setting fruit.

Thou shalt water in the cool of the evening so plants can sufficiently supply themselves with water before the next day's heat: Particularly if you know the following day will be very hot, your plants will appreciate getting a good drink the night before so they have stores of water to draw on to get through the day ahead. It's not uncommon for plants to wilt in the middle of very hot days; if they return to their normal shape when it's cooler out in the evening, they're ok. If they're still wilted come nightfall, provide extra water.

Thou shalt restrict watering to the roots and base of the plant: Try to not water leaves as much as possible. Leaves can develop diseases if left wet overnight; if watered during the heat of the day, they can burn.

Thou shalt not over water: Give it a minute to seep into the soil before drowning your plants and waterlogging your roots.

Thou shalt water plants evenly, otherwise soil will be displaced and root growth could be uneven: It's one of the cardinal sins of gardening to water your plants with so much pressure that the soil becomes displaced. Water with a gentle stream, and water evenly so the roots grow evenly.

ADDITIONAL STRATEGIES TO RETAIN MOISTURE

Retain moisture with compost: If you have very loose, sandy soil, you'll have a harder time keeping nutrients available for your plants. Rainwater will strip your topsoil of most nutrients. But soil with lots of organic matter like compost slows down the transition of water from the topsoil to the subsoil.

Let plants grow closer together: Gardeners throughout the centuries have relied on the Three Sisters for a reason: plants grown closer together conserve moisture, keep the ground cool, and keep weeds from sprouting. While you don't want to crowd your plants, consider planting them closer together, as you would if you were square foot gardening.

Mulch, mulch, mulch: Mulch helps retain water and prevent loss, as well as reduce the amount of weeds that might suck up water meant for your vegetables. Straw works well (and it's compostable). Add mulch to your garden just after watering.

Bush varieties = water conservation: Plants that spread or grow upwards lose more water faster than varieties that grow closer to the ground. Planting bush beans or cucumbers means less moisture lost to the air.

Add a drip system: Drip systems are fairly easy to build, require less water than other watering solutions, and can keep your garden healthy during the hottest days of summer.

Remove plants that aren't producing: Remove any spent or unproductive plants from your garden so water can be used by plants that are growing food for you.

WATERING SCHEDULE BASED ON VEGETABLE TYPE:

Plant	Water required per week (in gallons)
Beans	2
Beets	1
Broccoli	1
Brussels sprouts	1
Cabbage	2
Carrots	1
Cauliflower	2
Celery	2
Corn	2
Cucumbers	1
Leafy Greens	2
Onions	1
Parsnips	1
Peas	2
Potatoes	2
Squash	1
Tomatoes	2

Chapter 14: Homegrown Organic Fertilizers Rebel-Style

Unlike commercial synthetic fertilizers, organic fertilizers don't feed the plants directly. Instead, they add essential nutrients to the soil where they become available to the plants, more slowly, over time. While there's lots of different options for organic fertilizers, we'll only discuss a few options in this section for the sake of simplicity. By far, the simplest option is to reuse banana peels. If you have chickens, making chicken manure tea is a second simple option.

Understanding how fertilizers work

Before we get started, let's first look at how fertilizers work, which means understanding N-P-K. The N is for nitrogen, the P for phosphorus, and the K for Potassium. Each has an important role to play in the health of your garden, and understanding how to read the N-P-K means you'll be able to make your own fertilizers more effectively.

Nitrogen: Plants use nitrogen to grow tall, with lots of lush, leafy growth. If you examine the labels of most commercial fertilizers, you will find they have a high N-P-K ratio, including a high amount of nitrogen.

Phosphorus: Phosphorus helps plants grow strong and healthy roots, and promotes healthy flowering—necessary for your plants to set fruit.

Potassium: Potassium helps your garden with protein production, resisting diseases and insects, and using water effectively. Plants without enough potassium grow slower than normal, and can have yellow leaves.

Now that you understand how N-P-K works, let's talk about how you can make your own fertilizers for your organic garden.

Using Banana Peels

Banana peels are a rich source of nutrients your plants crave: Potassium, phosphorus, and calcium, along with a host of other minerals your plants need. Here's some simple ways to use leftover banana peels as fertilizer.

Banana Peel Tea:

This fertilizer uses nutrients leached from banana peels to give your plants a mineral boost. To make it, fill a mason jar with water, and add a banana peel. Let it sit for 48 hours. After 2 days, discard the peel (using one of the other methods in this article, hopefully!), leaving the water in your mason jar. Water your plants as usual with your banana tea.

Part 4: Nurturing Your Garden Organic Rebel Style

CHOP THE PEELS, THEN ADD TO YOUR GARDEN'S SOIL DIRECTLY:

Chop your banana peels into 1/4 inch pieces. Bury them before planting your vegetables at that location, or where you aren't in danger of hitting your plants' roots. As the peels decompose, all the valuable vitamins in the peels will reach the roots, giving you plants a nutrient bump that will make them happy.

GRIND THEM INTO A FERTILIZER:

Dry your banana peels (dry in the oven at 140 degrees, leaving the oven door open 1-2 inches). Once dry, grind the peels in a coffee or spice grinder. Add to your garden soil directly, either by sprinkling as a side dressing or gently incorporating into the dirt, making sure to avoid your plants' roots.

FERMENT PEELS FOR BIGGER BLOOMS:

Put your peels in a mason jar, and cover with enough water so they're submerged. Use a fermenting weight (http://thefrugalchicken.com/weight so your peels remain under water. Use an airlock kit to ferment (http://thefrugalchicken.com/lock).

Let the mixture sit for a week while the good bacteria does its job and unlocks the nutrients in the peel. If you see a cloudy must, that's ok. If you start to see black mold, you'll have to throw it away and start again. As long as the peels are below the surface of the water, you're probably okay. Let your nose and your judgement be your guide. After a week, put the peels in a blender and puree (save the water for other plants). Side dress your blossoming plants with the puree.

Banana peel vinegar (for acidic soil-loving plants):

This is good for blueberries. To create banana vinegar, follow the steps above to ferment the peels. After a week, remove the peels, and allow the water to sit, covered, until the mixture ferments into a vinegar. This can take anywhere from 4-6 weeks, depending on conditions such as temperature.

Let your nose tell you when it's turned to vinegar—it will have that unmistakable vinegar scent. If the mixture seems especially potent (you'll know by the scent), dilute it with water right before using so you don't accidentally burn your plants.

Chicken manure tea

If you have chickens, making manure tea is a good way to use up their waste and get even more benefit from your feathered friends. To a burlap bag (or other type of bag that can drain), add composted chicken manure. Add enough to the bag to fill up about a 1/3rd of it. Add something heavy, like a rock, into the bag to ensure it will stay submerged. Tie the bag closed.

Place into a 5-gallon bucket, and fill the bucket with water. Place the bucket in a sunny location outside to steep. A couple times each day, briskly stir the tea with a stick.

After about one week, your chicken manure tea should be ready. Remove the bag, and return the leftover manure to your compost pile or incorporate into another area of your garden to enhance that soil.

After removing the bag, fill the rest of the bucket up with fresh water. You want to get as close to a 1 to 1 ratio (1 part water to

1 part chicken manure tea) as possible. Give it to your plants every two weeks or so, pouring it gently onto the bottom of the plant so it hits the roots and doesn't displace the soil. Once your plants begin to flower and set fruit, only provide the chicken manure tea if they seem to need extra nutrients (for example, if it's very hot and the plant is stressed).

Rabbit manure

Up to 4 times more nutrient-rich than horse or cow poop, and twice as nitrogen-rich as chicken waste, rabbit manure doesn't need to be composted, and you can put it on your plants directly. It's high in nitrogen (approximately 2 percent), potassium (1 percent) and phosphorus (1 percent), and a great way to use something you'd otherwise throw away. A single buck (male) with two does (females) will produce at least two cubic yards of nutrient-manure you can spread in your garden to grow healthy vegetables.

Seed meal fertilizer

If you don't have access to manure, you can make your own seed meal fertilizer. This will invariably cost more than using manure, however.

Ingredients:

- ❏ 3 parts alfalfa meal or cottonseed meal.
- ❏ 1/4 part agricultural lime (http://thefrugalchicken.com/lime)
- ❏ 1/4 part gypsum (http://thefrugalchicken.com/gypsum)

- ❏ 1 part bone meal (http://thefrugalchicken.com/bonemeal)

Mix thoroughly in a wheelbarrow. A hoe will mix it easiest. You can find seed meal at grain dealers. The other ingredients can be found online. To use, side dress your plants when they flower and set fruit.

Seaweed fertilizer

This is a good recipe if you live near the ocean and have lots of seaweed available (or you don't mind buying it off the internet at http://thefrugalchicken.com/seaweed). Grab a 5 gallon bucket and add 7 cups of chopped seaweed. Fill the bucket halfway with water. Let the seaweed steep for 2 to 3 weeks. Strain the seaweed out, leaving the "tea." To use, combine water and seaweed fertilizer in equal parts and water your plants with it.

Homemade Fish Emulsion Fertilizer

You can easily make homemade fish emulsion fertilizer—a great source of nutrients for your garden—from leftover fish parts. If you're into fishing, you likely have fish parts and innards available. Be warned: The smell can be overwhelming, but on the other hand, you can reuse something you might otherwise throw away. In a 5 gallon bucket, combine 2 parts water with 1 part fish waste. Allow to steep for 24 hours. Add water until the bucket is full, leaving 2 to 3 inches of headroom. Cover and allow to ferment for 2 to 4 weeks. Once fermented, use like a compost tea on your plants.

Chapter 15:
Bee Cool:
Attracting Pollinators

Humans have known for ages that attracting beneficial pollinators to your garden means a larger harvest—and that's because these insects increase pollination and help ensure your plants will set fruit. Pollination occurs when pollen is transferred from one flower to a second flower of the same species. Although some plants can pollinate themselves, such as fig trees, most require the help of pollinators to start the process of fruit and seed production.

In fact, if your cucumber or squash plants fail to produce veggies or their veggies are tiny, it's likely because they weren't pollinated well enough. To improve your chances at a bountiful harvest, then attracting pollinators should be a top priority! When planning your garden, include some flowers to attract bees and butterflies, and be sure to locate the flowers close to your garden so pollinators will visit your vegetable plants too.

Bees

Know which beneficial bees are found in your area

Be sure to do some research to find out which bee species can be found in your area so you can have a strategic plan to attract them to your garden.
Since not all bees are searching for pollen at the exact same time, understanding which insects are local to your area and when they're active will determine which flowers you will plant to attract them. You can find this information on the internet or with your local agricultural extension.

Plant bee-friendly flowers

To attract pollinators, start by planting flowers that will draw them to your garden. Native wildflowers are a good option to attract local wild bees. Bees and flowers evolved together and have a symbiotic relationship, and flowers that attract local bees will be an excellent and regular source of pollen. Since not all bees are active at the same time of the season, be sure to plant flowers that will bloom throughout the warm months to continually attract our flying friends. Blue, purple and yellow flowers are the most appealing to bees.

Provide housing materials for bees

You can help establish bees in your garden by providing materials for wild bees to make their own hives. Bees use brush, dry grasses, and dead wood to make hives in the wild. Of course, another option is to install a commercial beehive and purchase bees or hope a wild swarm moves in. A bee house (http://thefrugalchicken.com/beehouse) is another option.

Flowers that attract bees

- ☐ Alyssum
- ☐ Anise hyssop
- ☐ Butterfly weed
- ☐ Aster
- ☐ Bee balm
- ☐ Black-eyed Susan
- ☐ Clover
- ☐ Echinacea (coneflower)
- ☐ Geranium
- ☐ Poppies

Essential oils to attract bees

If you use essential oils in your home, you can use them to attract beneficial insects like bees. A go-to oil that bees love is orange. Other options are lavender, marjoram, helichrysum, basil, sage, and rosemary. You can use any brand you like, just make sure it's pure essential oil from a brand you trust. If you want a recommendation, you can get started with the brand I endorse at http://thefrugalchicken.com/doTERRA. Don't place oils directly on any surfaces a bee might land on; a rag soaked in diluted oils (try a single drop diluted in 8 ounces of water) and hung up will suffice. Some oils, such as orange, can damage a bee's exoskeleton if too much of the oil comes in contact with the insect.

Butterflies

Butterflies are another group of pollinators that will benefit your organic garden. When designing your garden to attract these colorful visitors, keep in mind that you will want to include flowers that help butterflies at every stage of its life, including providing a place to lay eggs, offering food plants for caterpillars, creating places for the insects to form their chrysalides, as well as flowers that provide nectar for adult butterflies.

Know which butterflies are native to your region

Just like bees, you should know which butterfly species are already in your neighborhood if you want to attract these colorful pollinators to your garden. You can search for the specific butterfly species that are native to your local area at http://www.butterfliesandmoths.org/checklists.

Plant native flowers

Just like bees, planting native flowers that butterflies have used throughout history is the simplest way to attract them to your garden. You can find an extensive list of native plants categorized by region and state at http://www.wildflower.org/collections/.

Part 4: Nurturing Your Garden Organic Rebel Style

Red, yellow, pink, orange, and purple flowers will attract adult butterflies. Be sure to locate any flowering plants intended for butterflies in the sun since the insects will generally feed only in the sun. Make sure you plant flowers that will bloom in every season, since different butterfly species have different needs at different times of the year. One idea is to stagger your blooms to that when one type of flower dies, another species becomes available.

Flowers That Attract Adult Butterflies

- ❏ Alyssum
- ❏ Aster
- ❏ Bee balm
- ❏ Butterfly bush
- ❏ Calendula
- ❏ Daylily
- ❏ Delphinium
- ❏ Fennel
- ❏ Goldenrod
- ❏ Lavender
- ❏ Liatris
- ❏ Marigold
- ❏ Nasturtium
- ❏ Oregano

- ❏ Parsley
- ❏ Queen Anne's lace
- ❏ Sage
- ❏ Sunflowers
- ❏ Thyme
- ❏ Verbena
- ❏ Yarrow
- ❏ Zinnia

ESSENTIAL OILS TO ATTRACT BUTTERFLIES

Some essential oils will lure butterflies to your garden, including lavender, fennel, dill, helichrysum, thyme, and sage. If you attract butterflies with oils, be sure to be a good host and have nectar and water available for them so their visit is worthwhile for them. You can use any brand you like, just make sure it's pure essential oil from a brand you trust. If you want a recommendation, you can get started with the brand I endorse at http://thefrugalchicken.com/doTERRA.

PROVIDE AN ENVIRONMENT FOR CATERPILLARS

Unlike caterpillars that will damage your garden, butterfly caterpillars will leave your growing vegetables alone. Without these beneficial caterpillars, you won't have any adult pollinators, so provide the right plants (also called host plants) for immature butterflies to eat to ensure you'll have an adult population. In many cases, caterpillars of a particular butterfly species feed on only a very limited variety of plants. In this chapter is a list of common butterfly caterpillars and their host plants. For an indepth discussion, a great book is *The Family Butterfly Book* by Rick Mikula (http://thefrugalchicken.com/FamilyButterflyBook).

PROVIDE WATER & RESTING PLACES

Butterflies like to gather on wet sand and mud to drink water and glean minerals. This is known as "puddling." Create a place for butterflies in your garden to puddle with water offered in a shallow pan with moist sand.

COMMON BUTTERFLY CATERPILLARS AND THEIR HOST PLANTS (HTTP://THEFRUGALCHICKEN.COM/BUTTERFLYSEEDS):

Adult Butterfly Species	Native Region (North America Only)	Caterpillar Host Plant
Monarch (*Danaus plexippus*)	North America	Milkweed (Asclepias)
Anise Swallowtail (*Papilio zelicaon*)	Western North America	Anise, parsley, carrot, dill, fennel, rue
Black Swallowtail (*Papilio polyxenes*)	North America	Parsley, carrot, dill, fennel, rue
Eastern Tiger Swallowtail (*Papilio glaucus*)	Eastern North America	Lilac, willow, birch, tuliptree, cherry
Giant Swallowtail (*Papilio cresphontes*)	North America	Citruses, prickly ash, rue
Pipevine Swallowtail (*Battus philenor*)	North America	Dutchman's Pipe, pipevines, Virginia snakeroot
Spicebush Swallowtail (*Papilio troilus*)	North America east of Nebraska	Spicebush, sassafras, camphor tree (Cinnamomum camphora)
Checkered White (*Pontia protodice*)	North America	Crucifers, Cleome
Clouded Sulfur (*Colias philodice*)	North America (except CA & FL)	Clovers and other legumes
American Painted Lady (*Vanessa virginiensis*)	North America	Daisies, everlastings, Hollyhock (Alcea rosea)
Painted Lady (*Vanessa cardui*)	North America	Malva sylvestris, Tree mallow (Lavatera), thistles, goosefoots

Part 4: Nurturing Your Garden Organic Rebel Style

Adult Butterfly Species	Native Region (North America Only)	Caterpillar Host Plant
Red Admiral (*Vanessa atalanta*)	North America	Nettle, false nettle (Boehmeria cylindrica), hop
Pearly Crescentspot (*Phyciodes tharos*)	North America (except West Coast)	Asters, New England Aster (A. novae-angliae)
Common Buckeye (*Junonia coenia*)	North America (except Northwest)	Plantain, snapdragon, stonecrop, verbena, (Verbena bonariensis), other garden flowers
Spring Azure (*Celastrina ladon*)	North America (except Texas coastline, southern plains, and Florida peninsula)	Blueberry, California lilac, dogwoods, meadowsweet, viburnums
Viceroy (*Limenitis archippus*)	North America	Willow, poplar, aspen, apple, cherry, plum
Gulf Fritillary or Passion Butterfly (*Agraulis vanillae*)	Gulf regions of the United States	Passion flowers, Passiflora incarnata, Passiflora caerulea
Great Spangled Fritillary (*Speyeria cybele*)	North America	Violets, (Viola tricolor)
Variegated Fritillary (*Euptoieta claudia*)	North America (except Pacific Northwest)	Violets, (Viola tricolor), pansies, stonecrops, passion flowers (Passiflora incarnata), plantains
Gray Hairstreak (*Strymon melinus*)	North America (Continental US)	Cotton, strawberry, legumes, mints

Chapter 16: Self-Sufficient Water With Rain Barrels

Installing rain barrels is one way to conserve water while having clean water free of chemicals available for your garden. We try to conserve rainwater on our farm, especially since we've lived on properties that required an electric well pump—and when the electricity was out, guess what! No water! In this chapter, we'll cover how to choose, install, and use rain barrels.

There are several state and local governments that have banned water catchment, so the first thing you need to do before buying a rain barrel is check to see if you can legally own one. You may also want to check with your homeowner's association as well.

WHAT TO LOOK FOR IN A RAIN BARREL

SIZE

You want a sturdy, watertight rain barrel made of wood or food-safe plastic that will hold at least 50 gallons, because just a 1/10 of an inch of rain on a 1000 square foot roof will produce about 62 gallons of water.

OVERFLOW

Check that your potential rain barrel has an overflow. You are interrupting your guttering system to install the barrel, and the guttering is in place to protect your foundation. If the barrel doesn't have an overflow that allows you to redirect the water where you want it, then when the barrel overflows, *and it will overflow,* it will just puddle around your foundation. The overflow will also allow you to connect another rain barrel later.

SHAPE

If you are going to place the rain barrel against the wall, having an overly round barrel puts the catchment hole further from your guttering. Consider a flat-backed rain barrel.

CATCHMENT

Look to see what type of catchment it has and if it will suit your needs. If you have a guttering that you want to attach to, most commercial rain barrels are designed for that. But if you have a valley pitch in your roof that directs water to flow like Niagara Falls when it rains, you will need a different barrel. In that case, look for a barrel that has an open screened top, or a barrel that you can easily cut off the top.

Spigot

Where is the spigot located? The spigot needs to be located on the bottom of the barrel, otherwise you will never be able to use all the water in you barrel.

Installing Your Rain Barrel

You need a level foundation for your barrel. Depending on the size, rain barrels can weigh over 500 lbs when full and can be dangerous if you're anywhere near when it tips over.

Elevate the Rain Barrel For Water Pressure

Once you've leveled the ground, you need to elevate the barrel for water pressure as well as easier access to the faucet. Again, for safety reasons don't build it higher than your knee. Make sure your platform is stable! You can stack 16" square pavers, or build something. There are lots of great ideas on YouTube.

Cutting the Downspout On Your Gutters

You will need to cut the downspout about 4 to 6 inches above the barrel, AFTER you have leveled, built a platform, and placed your barrel on top. If you decided on a round barrel or you've cut it a little too high, just buy a flexi-downspout. A flexi-downspout is like an accordion, and will allow you some room to work it out.

Hoses For Your Rain Barrel

The handiest item you can have is a hose quick connect. One end permanently screws onto your rain barrel's spigot, and the other onto your hose.

Adding Mosquito Dunks To Protect Your Water

If your barrel is open at all, you will need to add mosquito dunks. These dunks contain BT, which is a naturally occurring soil bacteria called Bacillus thuringiensis. While it doesn't deter mosquitos, it does kill their larvae. Cut each ring into quarters, and use one quarter every month during the summer.

Chapter 17: Something Different: Using Essential Oils for Companion Planting

In some cases, you might want the benefits of companion planting without planting a particular herb. In those circumstances, you can use essential oils in your garden to get the benefit of companion planting. Similarly, if a particular plant won't grow in your area (for example, your growing season is too short or too hot, or if your soil isn't the right type, or your backyard doesn't get enough sun), or you have a small space and don't want an invasive species like peppermint to crowd your vegetables, you can still enhance your garden and aid the vegetables you CAN grow by "companion planting" with essential oils.

When using oils, also refer to Chapter 5: The Organic Rebel's Companion Planting Guide to make sure you aren't accidentally using an oil incompatible with another plant. There are a few herbal oils that are "universal oils," meaning their presence can benefit all the plants growing in your garden. These oils include basil, thyme, marjoram, and sage. (Additionally, you can use essential oils to attract beneficial insects to your garden or repel pests. See Chapter 15: Bee Cool: Attracting Pollinators.)

Mixing oils to use in your garden

The best way to use essential oils for companion planting is to combine the oils with water to dilute them. From there, you can either create a foliar spray or water particular plants with the essential oil/water combination directly in the soil. Simply combine 10 drops of essential oil with 6 quarts of water, stir vigorously since water and oil don't mix well, and use immediately.

With oils, less is more since they are so potent; you don't want to burn your plants with peppermint or overwhelm them by applying too much oil. Test essential oils on a single plant in your garden before spraying. If your plants respond well, then continue.

Be sure to use only pure oils from a brand you trust; the last thing you want is to work hard growing organic vegetables, only to introduce toxins from inferior, diluted oils into your garden. If you're looking for a brand recommendation, head to http://thefrugalchicken.com/doTERRA.

Part 4: Nurturing Your Garden Organic Rebel Style

Guide to Vegetable & Essential Oil Companions

Vegetable	Essential Oil Companion
Asparagus	Basil, Thyme
Beans	Lavender, Basil, Thyme
Broccoli	Basil, Thyme, Roman Chamomile
Brussels Sprouts	Peppermint, Spearmint, Rosemary, Clary Sage, Dill, Thyme
Cabbage	Peppermint, Thyme, Clary Sage
Carrots	Clary Sage, Basil, Rosemary, Marjoram
Cucumbers	Clary Sage, Basil, Marjoram
Eggplant	Basil, Clary Sage, Marjoram, Oregano
Kale	Basil, Thyme
Lettuce	Dill, Basil, Oregano
Onion	Roman Chamomile, Dill
Peas	Geranium, Basil, Marjoram
Peppers	Basil, Marjoram, Oregano, Thyme
Potatoes	Basil, Sage
Radishes	Dill, Basil
Spinach	Basil, Thyme, Oregano, Marjoram
Tomatoes	Basil, Oregano

Chapter 18: Easier Gardening with Hay Bales

Organic gardening isn't limited to planting in soil; you can also plant in other mediums, including hay and straw. Hay bale gardening can give you great yields, and it can make harvesting veggies much easier. Additionally, it cuts down on the amount of weeds, and as the hay deteriorates, it leaves rich compost behind.

What is hale bale gardening?

Hay bale gardening is essentially planting seeds into bales of hay instead of directly into the soil. Think of it like raised beds, but instead of using wood and soil, you're creating a naturally raised bed. And similarly, it prevents pests from damaging your crop. Not only is this method fun, it is painlessly easy because it requires very little upkeep. It also means easier harvesting because you don't have to bend over very far to grab your tomatoes or peppers!

How to Prepare Your Hay Bale Garden

Once you have decided to give hay bale gardening a go, your first step is to acquire hay bales if you do not yet have any. It's best to go with regular-sized 40 pound bales. Since freshness isn't really as much of an issue with hay for gardening as it is for animals, you can either buy your hay OR ask around to see if anyone is willing to give you old hay for free. Lots of times farmers are looking to clear space and might just give you rotting bales or will sell them to you at a discount.

Assemble the hay bales in your yard according to how you want your garden laid out. Once you have assembled the hay bales, you will want to begin the process of ensuring there aren't any stray seeds in your hay. To effectively get rid of any stray seeds, you'll want to introduce an organic fertilizer that's high in nitrogen into your bales. Instead of using a commercial high-nitrogen fertilizer, there's a simpler, more organic option: Urine.

Because you're starting the composting process quickly, it's possible that the temperature inside the hay bales can reach up to 140 degrees Fahrenheit. This can introduce a slight fire hazard, so when planning your garden layout, keep this in mind! If things get too heated, wet your bales every day, and if you want to be super safe, you can do it proactively. If you use the plastic or tarp, it's ok to remove it to wet the bales. You will know the process is complete when the temperature of the hay bales has returned to normal.

Planting your hay bale garden

Once your hay bales are conditioned, you're ready to plant seeds in them! This is probably the easiest part of the whole process. Just take your seeds and plant them into the hay bales. From that point, all you need to do to help them grow is to continue to keep the hay bales watered once every day. You should have a wonderful yield of tasty produce to collect at the end of the growing season, and as an added bonus, you can recycle the used hay bales as fresh compost for your other gardens or plant beds!

Chapter 19: Weed Control, Organic Rebel-Style

Weeds can be an organic gardener's curse. Actually, for all gardeners, weeds are the bane of their existence in some cases. There really is no easy answer to this problem. It just takes time and effort to control the unwanted overgrowth in your garden.

OPTIONS FOR ORGANIC WEED CONTROL

NEWSPAPER OR CARDBOARD

In a study performed at the University of Vermont, researchers found that a 6-inch layer of shredded newspaper prevented weeds from growing. You can also use cardboard, since newspaper has been printed with ink. To use newspaper or cardboard for weed control, place it on the ground in your garden. Layer 6 inches of dirt and compost over the newspaper or cardboard, and evenly distribute. If you don't want to dig up your garden, then you can simply place 4 or 5 layers of newspaper in between your plants and cover with a light layer of dirt.

Mulch

One of the easiest ways to control weeds with with a thick layer of mulch that keeps light from reaching weeds and nourishes your plants as it decomposes. Examples of organic mulches include straw, grass clippings, or leaves. Straw works well because you can be relatively assured there's not many seeds in it to cover your garden with weeds. Another option is woodchips or sawdust, although they will leach nitrogen as they decompose.

Before installing mulch, first establish your transplants and water well. Then gently spread 3 to 4 inches of mulch around them, and water consistently. Be warned that if you use grass clippings or leaves, you run the risk of bringing insects or diseases into the garden if these are not composted.

There are two potential pitfalls to mulching. One is to mulch heat-loving plants too early in the season, before the soil warms up. Another mistake is to put down too little mulch. It looks good for a few weeks, but then weeds poke through, and they must be hand pulled. In addition, insufficient mulch also gives your plants much less drought protection.

So how much is enough?

- ❑ Sawdust, 2 to 3 inches
- ❑ Shredded leaves, 8 to 10 inches
- ❑ Straw, 5 to 7 inches

- ❏ Newspaper, 6 inches
- ❏ Grass clippings, 5 inches

Landscape Fabric

If you live in a wet climate, you may wish to avoid mulching because mulch can lead to waterlogged soil and fungal diseases. If your garden is relatively small, black landscape fabric is a good option. (http://thefrugalchicken.com/landscapefabric) Like mulch, the fabric will prevent weeds from getting light.

It can be expensive, but it's better than hoeing or pulling weeds continuously throughout the summer. Place the landscape fabric over you composted garden, making sure to tack it down. When your seedlings are ready to transplant, cut holes in the fabric so you can bury the plants in the soil.

Hoeing

If you need to get rid of weeds that have already grown, using a hoe is an option. When stuck just below the surface of the soil and severed from their roots, weeds will die. Twice a week, run the edge of a sharp hoe just under the surface of the soil to behead tiny weeds before they grow large enough to compete with your seedlings. Be aware that weeds will likely grow back, so if possible, prevent weeds rather than having to get rid of them after your plants are established.

Hand Weeding

If your plants are too close for hoeing, then hand weeding is an easy option. It's best to tackle weeds when they're young and haven't developed a tough root system yet. Gloves and a sitting pad are necessary to ensure your comfort if you will be weeding for a while. If the day is hot, also bring a water bottle so you stay hydrated; it's best to pull weeds in the early morning or evening if you will be doing it for a while. Consider weeding after you have watered since they will slide out of the soil easier when the soil is wet. To keep weeds from returning, pull the root out as well.

If you're feeling particularly sneaky, one method is to encourage weeds to grow *before* you plant your garden by warming up the soil with clear plastic. Once sprouted, pull them out by their roots.

Organic weed control spray

Finally, organic weed control can be done easily by placing common household vinegar in a spray bottle and apply it to weeds. Be careful when applying around your vegetable plants, however, because it's very potent. To make this spray, add ¼ cup of vinegar to a quart of water. Shake well to mix.

Chapter 20: Organic Pest Control

For the natural gardener, pest control might seem like a daunting task. After all, you're committed to not using harmful chemicals in your garden, yet these chemicals can get rid of pests quickly and easily. There are still many ways you can take control of your garden without resorting to chemical treatments. Natural pest control is actually quite easy, and you have a lot of options. Far and away, however, it's better to prevent pests than to try to get rid of them. In this chapter, we'll discuss both.

Options for Organic Pest Control

Row Cover or Hoop House

The main advantage to row covers is you can protect your plants from insects without needing any sort of spray. Row covers act as an insect barrier, while still letting in the sunlight. They're best when supported by PVC hoops to allow air to circulate around the plants instead of merely covering them. When purchasing fabric for row covers, note first the width of your garden beds. Fabric can be 60" wide and up to 8 feet wide.

Row covers are easy to make. After you've purchased the fabric, you can drape it over a PVC frame. You can either push the ends of the PVC into the soil (which isn't very sturdy) or stabilize them with rebar stakes. A simple solution if you use raised beds is to install inserts on the wood to hold the PVC in place. You will also need to secure the fabric on either side of the bed and to the PVC to prevent it blowing away in the wind.

Row covers are a good temporary option to help seedlings or during times when pests are more likely to harm a particular plant species. If your plant requires insects for pollination, then at flowering times, this isn't the best option.

NEEM OIL

Neem oil (http://thefrugalchicken.com/neem) is a popular defense against pests with organic gardeners. It's a vegetable oil pressed from the fruits and seeds of the neem (*Azadirachta indica*), an evergreen tree which is native to the Indian subcontinent. Neem oil is so popular because while it doesn't harm mammals and beneficial insects, it repels mealybugs, beet armyworm, aphids, the cabbage worm, thrips, whiteflies, mites, fungus gnats, beetles, moth larvae, mushroom flies, leafminers, caterpillars, locust, nematodes and the Japanese beetle.

Sticky Traps

Sticky traps attract specific insects based on the colors they're attracted to. These are an option, however, note that in order to work, the traps must be clean and sticky. You can buy them commercially (http://thefrugalchicken.com/stickytraps) or make them yourself.

How to make a sticky trap

To make them, identify which colors will attract the insects you want to eliminate, and use cardboard or plastic. White or yellow work with most garden pests. Cut them to 4 inches by 6 inches and paint it the correct color. Line the trap with plastic wrap and coat with a clear, sticky substance (corn syrup and petroleum jelly are two options). When spent, remove the plastic wrap, toss, and line the trap with plastic again. If you don't want to use plastic, you can use any other liner, or use colored paper to create the traps then compost when spent.

Insecticidal Soap

Commercial insecticidal soaps work by dissolving the hard external bodies of insects. They're effective against aphids, thrips, mites, immature leafhoppers, and whiteflies. While these are an option, they're only effective if they come in contact with the insects while still a liquid. It won't work after it dries on the plants. You also run the risk of damaging beneficial insects or burning some plant leaves. To make your own, combine 5 tablespoons of pure castile liquid soap (without any fragrances or colors) to 2 quarts of water. Combine thoroughly and use immediately.

Beneficial Organisms

Bacillus Thuringiensis

Bacillus thuringiensis is a naturally-occurring bacterium found in the soil. You can buy it commercially (http://thefrugalchicken.com/BT), and it's effective against many different species of pests, including cabbage loopers, tomato hornworms, cabbage worms, Colorado potato beetles, corn borers, and squash vine borers. It works by releasing a protein after an insect consumes a plant sprayed with the bacterium, however, it's only effective when an insect actually eats it.

It's important to note that it's not effective against adult insects, so use it as soon as your plant is infested with larvae, and reapply every couple of days until you don't spot anymore larvae. Because the bacterium can kill beneficial insects, it's best to only spray it when you have a confirmed pest problem, and only spray the infested plants.

Parasitic Nematodes

You can purchase parasitic nematodes commercially (http://thefrugalchicken.com/parasiticnematodes), and they're a great organic option for parasite control if armyworms, corn earworms, squash vine borers, Japanese beetle larvae, weevils, root maggots, and cutworms are a problem in your garden. Once inside a pest, parasitic nematodes release bacteria that kills the insect host within a day or two.

Ladybugs

You can buy ladybugs by the pint, quart, or gallon (http://thefrugalchicken.com/ladybugs). The average-sized garden can get by on a quart or less, as there will be about 25 to 30 thousand bugs per quart. The cost is generally less than $5 a quart, and the average adult ladybug consumes between 40 and 50 aphids a day.

Praying Mantises

Praying mantis cases are also available and each one hatches up to 400 young (http://thefrugalchicken.com/prayingmantises). They will eat any insect they can catch.

Frogs

Frogs and lizards can also control pests by eating them. You can make your garden hospitable for them by keeping a water source available and by not wiping out the entire pest population with a pesticide, sending frogs elsewhere in search of food. You also can give them places to hide, for example a toad house (http://thefrugalchicken.com/toadhouse).

Guide to Preventing Pests Based on Species

It's also important to prevent pests based on species. Here's a guide to common insects that can destroy your plants, how to prevent them, and how to rid your garden of them should they invade:

Aphids

Aphids are tiny, pear-shaped insects. Some types of aphids have wings, and may be green, pink, yellowish, black, or powdery gray. Larvae resemble adults, but are smaller and wingless. They feed in colonies, so where there's one, there's more. Aphids feeding can cause leaves to curl and become deformed, killing the plant.

To deter: Plant mint or yarrow around your garden to attract aphid predators.

To get rid of: Pick them off and crush them or knock them from plants with a strong spray of water. Add ladybugs to your garden.

Potato Beetles

To deter: Rotate potato beds every year. Mulch with straw 6 inches deep around plants. Choose early-maturing potatoes so harvest is over before beetles mature. Hoe planting sites in fall to expose and kill adult potato beetles.

To get rid of: Handpick off plants and drop into soapy water. Knock orange-yellow eggs on leaf undersides off. Spray with Homemade Insect Spray (recipe follows).

Cutworm

To deter: Surround the stem of each transplant with a ring of rigid cardboard, 6 inches tall and dug 2 inches into the soil to prevent cutworms.

To get rid of: Mix bran with water and the bacterium Bacillus thuringiensis. Sprinkle mixture over your garden 7 days before planting.

Cabbageworm (Cabbage looper)

These pests are light green in color with white stripes running down their back. The larvae can reach approximately 1½ inches long, and feed between the veins on the undersides of leaves. Large larvae make ragged holes in the foliage and move to the center of the plant where feeding generally occurs at the base of the cabbage head. Large loopers can burrow through three to six layers of tightly wrapped head leaves.

To deter: Install a row cover or hoop house immediately after planting.

To get rid of: Find and knock off eggs on leaves (or spray with Homemade Insect Spray). Handpick caterpillars and deposit into soapy water. Spray with Bacillus thuringiensis.

Slugs
To get rid of:

Diatomaceous earth: Diatomaceous earth (http://thefrugalchicken.com/de) is a natural substance created from the fossilized remains of diatoms. It works against slugs because it's extremely sharp and cuts their undersides. Eventually, the slug becomes dehydrated and dies. Only use Food Grade diatomaceous earth, which you can find in garden centers.

Copper: Copper works as an effective slug deterrent because the moisture in the slug's body reacts with the copper, shocking the insect. You can lay the copper flat or create a short 2 inch fence around your plants.

Red Clover: Clover works because slugs are attracted to the clover, leaving your vegetables intact. You're also left with a nitrogen-heavy plant to compost.

Hand Picking: In the early morning and early evening during slug season, pluck as many slugs as you can find. Drop them in soapy water to kill them.

Squash Bugs

To deter: Use row covers or hoop houses until flowering. Choose squash bug resistant varieties.

To get rid of: Use wood boards and place next to plants. Squash bugs will hide under them. Handpick and place in soapy water. Gently scrape eggs off leaves or spray with All Natural Bug Spray.

Tomato Hornworms

Tomato hornworms are green caterpillars that can measure up to 4 inches in length. The prominent "horn" gives them their name. Hornworms are often difficult to see because of their protective coloring which is green. Not much for the heat of direct sunlight, they tend to feed on the interior of the plant during the day and are more easily spotted when they move to the outside of the plant at dawn and dusk.

To deter: Use row covers or cages.

To get rid of: The best way to control hornworms is to handpick them off your plants. They are also especially susceptible to Bacillus thuringiensis.

ALL-NATURAL BUG SPRAY

This recipe is an easy way to make your own organic bug spray. To use it, spray on your plant's leaves.

INGREDIENTS

- 1 garlic bulb
- 1 small red onion
- 1 teaspoon fresh cayenne pepper
- 1 quart of water
- 1 tablespoon liquid castile soap (http://thefrugal-chicken.com/castile)

Grind garlic and onion together in a blender. Add cayenne pepper and pour into in 1 quart water. Allow to steep for an hour. Strain out the garlic and onion. Add the castile soap. Shake to mix. Spray on plants thoroughly. Good for 10 days.

GARLIC PEST CONTROL SPRAY

Garlic pest control spray can be used to control cabbage worms, leafhoppers, squash bugs, whiteflies, but can also kill beneficial insects. Be careful when you apply it.

- 3 ounces finely chopped garlic
- 2 tsp mineral oil

- [ ] 1 pint water
- [ ] ¼ ounce liquid castile soap

To make the concentrate: Combine the garlic and mineral oil and allow to soak for 24 hours. The following day, add water and liquid castile soap. Stir and strain into a glass jar. When you're ready to use it, dilute 2 tablespoons of the garlic pest control spray in 1 pint of water. For some plants, this mixture can be quite strong, so be sure to test it on a single leaf before spraying the entire plant. Use this spray only when necessary.

ESSENTIAL OILS TO REPEL GARDEN PESTS

If you use essential oils in your home, you can also use them to rid your garden of unwanted pests that will try to steal your harvest. To employ essential oils to repel pests, you have some options. You can:

- [ ] Add 10 drops per 6 quarts of water and create a foliar spray. Be sure to double check the oil and your vegetable are good companions. (Chapter 17: Something Different: Using Essential Oils For Companion Planting).
- [ ] Add 6 drops of essential oil to clean rags and hang or place the rags in your garden, near the effected plants.
- [ ] Place containers with a few drops of oil near your plants.
- [ ] Craft candles by including a selected essential oil and burning the candles (similar to burning citronella candles to repel mosquitos).

Part 4: Nurturing Your Garden Organic Rebel Style

WHICH ESSENTIAL OIL TO USE?

If you're new to oils, or aren't sure which one will most benefit your garden, think about which plants in your garden are effected by the pests, and examine which oils are their natural companions to repel pests. Then, determine which pests are bothering your garden, and which oil will best repel them using the chart that follows. If more than one pest threatens your plant, or in insect AND a fungus are causing trouble, then it's perfectly fine to add more than one oil to water, to a rag, or to a container. If you want a go-to oil for killing insects, then orange is a good choice, since it works to destroy the exoskeletons of bugs. A second option is cedarwood, which is believed to interfere with their neurological capabilities. You can use your favorite brand, just be sue the oil is pure, and the oil in the bottle is as advertised. If you're looking for a brand recommendation, you can get started with the brand I trust at http://thefrugalchicken.com/doTERRA.

ESSENTIAL OILS TO REPEL PESTS

Pest	Essential Oil Known To Repel
Ants	Peppermint, Spearmint, Wild Orange, Cedarwood
Aphids	Peppermint, Spearmint, Cedarwood, Wild Orange
Beetles	Peppermint, Thyme, Wild Orange, Cedarwood
Caterpillars	Rosemary, Cedarwood
Cats	Rosemary
Cutworms	Thyme, Clary Sage, Cedarwood
Dogs	Black Pepper, Peppermint
Fleas	Lavender, Lemongrass, Peppermint, Wild Orange, Rosemary, Cedarwood
Flies	Lemongrass, Eucalyptus, Peppermint, Basil, Cedarwood
Fungus (e.g. Powdery Mildew)	Melaleuca, Wild Orange
Lice	Peppermint, Spearmint, Cedarwood
Rabbits, Mice	Peppermint
Slugs/Snails	Cedarwood, Douglas Fir, Peppermint
Squash Bugs	Peppermint, Wild Orange, Cedarwood

Part 4: Nurturing Your Garden Organic Rebel Style

PROTECTING YOURSELF WITH GARDENER'S DELIGHT ORGANIC FLY REPELLENT

If it's summer, it's bug season, and it's no fun trying to work in your garden if you're being harassed by insects. Here's a buy spray you can make at home with essential oils.

Ingredients

- ❏ 10 drops Lemongrass or Lavender for scent (or your favorite scent)
- ❏ 10 drops Eucalyptus
- ❏ 10 drops Peppermint

Slowly drip each oil into a 10mL roller bottle and top with a carrier oil such as fractionated coconut oil, almond oil, or avocado oil. To apply, roll the bug spray onto your neck, arms, and legs. You can use any brand you like. You can go to http://thefrugalchicken.com/doTERRA to get started with the brand I endorse. You can purchase roller bottles at http://thefrugalchicken.com/rollerbottle.

Part 5:
Gardening in the 4th Season

Chapter 21: Extending Your Growing Season

In Northern climates, extending your growing season means fresh organic veggies during times when you otherwise might have to rely on your canned harvest or going to the grocery store. Depending on your zone and whether you use a hot bed or not, you can extend your growing season by quite a bit. In our area, with cold frames, we can extend our growing season into January. With a hot bed, we can grow year round. The key is to test out different season-extending options to see what works for your area, and to remember that it's best to try to grow plants that can handle a cooler environment and less-than-optimal sunlight.

Cold Frames

A cold frame is simply a (usually) wood box with a transparent lid that raises the temperature inside using solar energy, so it provides a warmer environment for your crops. A cold frame works by trapping the sun's rays inside the box, heating the air and soil inside. The heat trapped inside is then released at night, and provides warmth for your growing greens. You can use a cold frame either in early spring or into winter, and use it to harden off tender seedlings before their final transplant in the garden.

Choosing a location

A choice site for your cold frame is in an area with a good Southern exposure in full sun, and with a windbreak. Placing your cold frame next to your house or protected by trees, bushes, or a wall are good options.

While you can build your cold frame on surface soil, a better option is to dig down 10 inches and locate the bottom of your cold frame deep into the earth. The temperature will be warmer and more stable. A site with good drainage will ensure water won't drown your plants during storms, or lower the overall temperature.

Constructing your cold frame
Materials needed:

- ☐ (1) 3- or 4-foot-long lid (a salvaged window, for example)
- ☐ (1) Cedar plank, cut to the length of the lid, 22 inches tall
- ☐ (1) Cedar plank cut to the length of the lid, 28 inches tall

- ☐ (2) Cedar planks cut to the width of the lid; one side of the planks should be 22 inches tall, the other side 28 inches tall
- ☐ Enough sturdy hinges to secure the lid to the cold frame
- ☐ (1) 5 pound box of 2-inch screws to construct the body of the cold frame
- ☐ Handles to lift the lid

Instructions:

To build your cold frame, first choose your lid. It can be an old glass window, a piece of thick food-safe plastic screwed to a wood frame, or anything else you can scrounge up for free that's in good condition and can be altered into a lid. Don't make it too wide, or you'll have a hard time tending to your plants. A width of 24 to 36 inches works well.

Your lid should also be fairly light weight; if it's too heavy, you will have difficulty hinging it to the body of your cold frame and lifting it. Making your cold frame 3 feet long works well; just remember, that the longer your cold frame is, the more energy it will have to trap to raise the interior temperature. If you have more plants than your cold frame can handle you can always build another one!

To build the body of your cold frame, choose wood that weathers well and will last you a long time. Cedar is a good choice, since the natural oils in it help it withstand the elements. The body of your cold frame should slope to help with water runoff during storms and to trap in the maximum amount of heat possible. An optimal height is 18 inches in the back, and sloping to 12 inches in the front. Be sure to apply weather stripping where the lid meets the frame to help your cold frame retain heat.

Maintaining an optimal temperature in your cold frame

The optimal temperature inside your cold frame will depend on what you're growing; for cool-weather greens such as kale, a maximum temperature of 50 degrees F will suffice; for warm-loving vegetables, 70 degrees F is best. It's best to keep a thermometer inside your cold frame so you can know exactly what the temperature is, and open the cold frame to ventilate it when the temperature gets too high. If you will be at work during the day, you can buy an automatic vent controller that will open and close the lid at a preset temperature. Similarly, if it will be below the optimal temperatures in your cold frame, a thermometer will alert you so you can drape a tarp on it before nightfall so you can provide extra insulation.

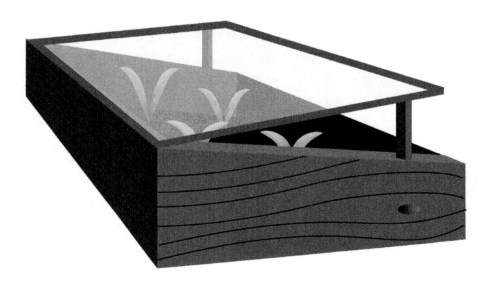

Vegetables & Temperatures to Apply Cold Frames

Vegetable	Possible damage if temp is under:
Asparagus	32
Beans	32
Beets	32
Bok Choy	35
Broccoli	30
Cabbage	28
Carrots	32
Kale	30
Peas	32
Potatoes	30
Radishes	32
Spinach	32

Overwintering Root Vegetables

If desired, you can overwinter carrots, kale, leeks, parsnips, radishes, spinach, and turnips for a continued harvest as long as the ground isn't frozen solid. Be sure to cover them with a thick layer of mulch or straw. Your garlic, if planted in the fall, will overwinter until the following spring. Mulch it with at least 4 inches of straw until temperatures rise the following spring.

Hot Beds

A hot bed is simply a cold frame that is heated, usually by adding fresh manure to the bottom of the cold frame. As the manure decomposes, it releases heat, which raises the temperature inside the cold frame. If manure isn't available, you can use a heat mat. Like a cold frame, you can choose a site for your hot bed with a good Southern exposure and with a windbreak.

How to make a hot bed

If you will use fresh manure to create your hot bed, instead of excavating 10 inches into the earth, as you would if you were just constructing the cold frame, instead dig 18 inches further. Construct your raised bed (adjusting the body measurements for the increased depth). Before affixing the lid to the cold frame, first fill the interior of the cold frame with 12 inches of fresh horse or cow manure. Allow the material to settle for a week, turning it and lightly spraying with water until it settles, then cover it with 6 inches of soil, then add the lid to the cold frame. As the manure decomposes, it will raise the temperature inside.

Chapter 22: Gardening Over Winter

As the days grow shorter, temperatures drop and there's less available light. But that doesn't mean the fun is over. Winter is just as important for your organic garden as every other season. After working hard to cultivate healthy soil for your plants, the last thing you want to do is just let it sit, and in the late fall, you can start creating a healthy environment for your next generation of plants. And believe it or not, you can also garden in winter! In this chapter, we'll look at how to care for your garden when harvest season is over and crops you can grow indoors and when the days are shorter.

Garden clean up

At the end of the fall, remove any remaining plants you don't plan to overwinter. Make note of where vegetables were planted so you can easily rotate crops in the spring.If the plants are disease-free, then you can compost them. If any are diseased, either burn them or throw them away. You don't want them contaminating your soil. Protect your compost pile with a thick layer of straw before a hard frost threatens. Prune raspberry bushes according to directions in Chapter 10: Fruits Of Your Labor and cover strawberry beds with 4 inches of straw or hay to protect them.

Till your garden to a depth of 4 inches to try to eliminate pests that plan to overwinter. This will reduce your pest load the following spring. Add a 3-inch layer of compost and cultivate till into the soil. You can also add fresh manure and allow it to rot over the winter.

Weed the garden before the ground freezes to reduce weeds the following spring, or, if desired, you can cover your entire garden or just certain areas with black plastic to eliminate weeds. Leave it there until temperatures rise again.

Place cold frames around plants you plan to overwinter, such as spinach or kale, before temperatures get too cold. Dig an area for a hotbed (Chapter 21: Extending Your Growing Season); if you plan to use it to grow leafy greens over winter, then add fresh manure.

COVER CROPS

Cover crops perform a number of vital tasks in your garden over the winter. With the right cover crops, you can add nutrients to your soil, as well as prevent the wind from scattering your precious topsoil everywhere. Examples of cover crops that will perform both tasks are red clover, alfalfa, Austrian peas, buckwheat, oats, ryegrass, and winter wheat. When you choose a cover crop, consider whether you will want to harvest it, or plan to till it into the soil so you can plant your spring crops.

Cover crops such as winter wheat can obviously be harvested for their seeds, however, wheat matures around June, which is quite late to be planting your spring crops. Other crops such as clover can simply be tilled into the soil whenever you're ready to plant your spring vegetables.

To grow a cover crop, direct sow seeds right after your fall harvest has ended. Most varieties need at least 4 weeks to establish themselves before a frost threatens.

Chapter 23: Growing Indoors

Even though the outdoors might be too chilly to grow anything, and the days too short, you can still provide fresh greens for your family indoors. You can use a sunny window established plants such as herbs; for bean or sunflower sprouts, very little light is needed.

HERBS

If you grew your herbs in pots, you can easily just transport them inside, and continue to feed them compost and harvest sprigs over the winter. Any herbs (except cilantro—its taproot is too long) that were directly planted in soil can be potted as well. If you have a grow light, pots, organic potting soil, and a relatively warm room (or a heat mat), you can germinate and grow your herbs indoors over the winter.

Sprouts

Sprouts are one crop you can grow pretty much anywhere, and they don't require much: A sprouting tray or mason jar, moisture, and heat. Sprouts are full of healthy vitamins, and because they're young and tender, the vitamins are more bioavailable than if you consumed just the seeds or the mature plant. Some common choices include alfalfa, beans, peas, lentils, pumpkin, sunflower, and chia.

How to grow sprouts

To grow sprouts in your kitchen, you will need:

- A wide-mouth quart mason jar
- A piece of cloth and rubber band to cover the mouth of the mason jar
- Organic sprouting seeds (http://thefrugalchicken.com/sprouts)

The amount of seeds you will use depends on the variety you choose. For smaller seeds, start with 1 tablespoon; for larger seeds, start with ¼ cup. If you end up using them quickly and want more available, then you can adjust the amount you start with. Place seeds in a mason jar. Cover the sprouts with 1 cup of water, and allow to soak overnight.

The following morning, strain the seeds from the water using a thin-mesh colander or cheesecloth. Rinse the seeds, and return to the mason jar. Allow the excess water to run off the seeds by placing the mason jar with the open end down at a slight angle. Rinse the sprouts each day, returning to the tilted position each time. Within 48 hours, you should see sprouting. When the first set of leaves have appeared, your sprout are ready to harvest. Rinse well, and add to a sandwich or salad. If you see mold at any point, throw the sprouts away and sterilize the mason jar.

If you are concerned about food-borne illnesses associated with sprouts, you can soak your harvested sprouts in 1 part lemon juice (or 1 drop of lemon essential oil) to 6 parts water for 15 minutes before sprouting before eating; the acidic nature of the lemon juice is said to help kill bacteria.

MICROGREENS

Microgreens are popular to grow because they don't cost very much and are packed with nutrients and beneficial enzymes. Essentially, they're the same as seedlings, but they're harvested sooner. Because they're right out of the seed, they're more tender and nutritious than the mature plant. You can grow anything as a microgreen, but popular choices include lettuce, kale, spinach, turnips, beets, radishes, chia, buckwheat, mustard, and cabbage. Unlike sprouts, microgreens are grown in soil.

HOW TO GROW MICROGREENS
SUPPLIES NEEDED:

- ❑ Seeds of your choosing (http://thefrugalchicken.com/microgreens)
- ❑ Shallow tray
- ❑ Organic potting soil (Chapter 7: Getting Ahead: Starting Seeds Indoors)
- ❑ Warming mat

❑ Grow lights (optional)

Pour and smooth 1 inch of your organic potting soil in your grow tray. Scatter the seeds as evenly as possible over the surface of the soil. Don't worry about spacing; because your microgreens will only grow to 1 inch tall at most, and you want to get as large of a harvest as possible, space isn't as much of a concern.

Cover the seeds with a thin layer of soil, and mist with water. Cover the grow tray with a plastic cover, and mist once every other day. If your room temperature is cool, use the warming mat to ensure soil temperatures will be at least 70 degrees to ensure the seeds actually sprout. Some seeds won't germinate if soil temperatures are too low. Alternatively, you can place the trays on top of your refrigerator, or any other place that's warm. Place the tray on a sunny windowsill, or even better, under grow lights. You will soon see sprouts appear. Harvest when greens reach 1 inch tall or sooner. To harvest, cut right above soil level with scissors or a sharp knife.

To grow microgreens again, fill the tray with more soil and repeat the above steps. You can compost the soil or reuse it; you will likely get some volunteer microgreens if you reuse the soil.

Organic Seed Sources

Baker Creek: http://www.rareseeds.com/

Seeds Now: http://thefrugalchicken.com/seedsnow (affiliate)

Seeds of Change: https://www.seedsofchange.com/

Grow Organic: https://www.groworganic.com/

Sustainable Seed Company: http://sustainableseedco.com

Seed Savers Exchange: http://www.seedsavers.org/

References

1. https://www.forbes.com/sites/alicegwalton/2015/03/21/monsanto-herbicide-dubbed-probably-carcinogenic-by-world-health-organization-are-they-right/#6913a90135e8

2. http://articles.latimes.com/2005/jan/01/nation/na-pest1

3. http://compost.css.cornell.edu/calc/cn_ratio.html

4. http://msue.anr.msu.edu/news/fall_fruiting_raspberry_varieties_for_2017

5. http://www.fruit.cornell.edu/mfruit/gooseberries.html

6. http://permaculturenews.org/2014/08/26/permanently-improve-sandy-soil/

7. https://www.intechopen.com/books/organic-farming-a-promising-way-of-food-production/quality-and-nutrient-contents-of-fruits-produced-under-organic-conditions

8. http://www.medicaldaily.com/monsanto-roundup-herbicide-cancer-non-hodgkins-lymphoma-386398

9. http://extension.psu.edu/plants/crops/esi/treated-lumber

Printed in Great Britain
by Amazon